FUTURE
SKILLS

FUTURE
SKILLS

PERTTU PÖLÖNEN

TRANSLATED BY OWEN F. WITESMAN

VIVA
EDITIONS

Published in the United States by Viva Editions, an imprint of Start
Midnight, LLC, 221 River Street, Ninth Floor, Hoboken, New Jersey
07030.

Printed in the United States
Cover design: Jennifer Do
Cover image: Shutterstock
Text design: Frank Wiedemann

First Edition.
10 9 8 7 6 5 4 3 2 1

Trade paper ISBN: 978-1-63228-074-9
E-book ISBN: 978-1-63228-131-9

To everyone I've learned from.

CONTENTS

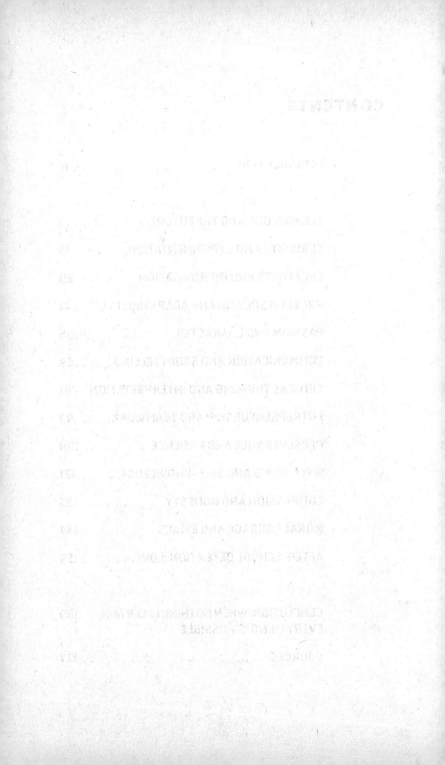

INTRODUCTION

What makes one person wiser than another? Once in kindergarten my friends and I, all about five years old, were faced with a difficult problem. As we had been going about our normal play, an unexplained hole had opened up in our worldview. Rushing to our teacher, Petri, we asked what makes a person wise. After considering this for a moment, he said that a person becomes wiser the more times he's been around the sun. Wisdom develops in the human brain as this circular motion continues, he said, and usually the older a person is, the more time they've had to rotate through different recurring patterns in life and in the natural world. It was all about circles. That's why parents are usually wiser than children.

We were entranced by this information. Rushing out into the yard, my friends and I spread our arms out wide and started spinning. We continued spinning for hours, believing that we were doing ourselves a great service. The more circles we turned, the wiser we were getting!

Now, almost twenty years later, I've learned that Petri

was right. The more time a person has spent looking around and seeing things from different perspectives during their life, the wiser they're likely to be. Whenever someone accuses me of being wise, I say that the fault is in my early childhood education and those hours of spinning.

There was also a second day when we found another hole in our view of the world—we didn't know why people die. This time Petri said that people have blood inside them and if the blood runs out, the person can't stay alive anymore. We didn't know that the human body is always making new blood, though, instead thinking that each of us only contained a set amount of blood. When I fell playing outside and scraped my knee, I froze in terror when I realized that precious blood was leaking out of me. I thought I was losing years of my life! The next time someone reminded me to be more careful, I knew that the adults just didn't want me to die prematurely from blood loss.

Petri was wrong that time, but so was I. We should never be afraid of small accidents and injuries, because we learn best from our mistakes. Sometimes people who experience setbacks and disappointments just get stronger. Sometimes it's the people who have to do the most catching up who go the farthest. Exertion doesn't weaken the heart, it strengthens it.

The skills of the future cannot be taught from teacher to student like multiplication tables or grammar. It's hard to make multiple-choice questions about courage or to assign points to a person's curiosity, even though these are very important skills. Many of the skills we will need in the future are learned through trial and error. Sometimes you have to change your assumptions, and sometimes you fail spectacularly. It's frustrating that recess is more important than class time for developing many skills and that after-hours gatherings are frequently more useful than team meetings.

This book isn't just for schoolchildren or college students—it's for all of us. We're in the midst of an unprecedented period of technological development, and we need lifelong learning at home and at work. We can't be sure what skills the future will demand of us, although expert predictions can provide some direction. If I were in charge, I would put a best-before date on all diplomas and certificates. At least one thing is clear: we will be required to continue to adapt to new innovations.

It's important to understand what changes we face at the individual and societal levels, but it is even more important to focus on what isn't changing. The wisest course of action is to develop now the skills that we will need throughout our lives. Currently we tend to value speed when what we really need is depth. The world needs to be made better, not just more efficient. We must continue to develop the human qualities that have always been important to us, because technological developments are likely to make them even more important in the future. In the midst of constant change, the most valuable thing isn't what is changing but what is not.

The idea for *Future Skills* came from pondering what schools should be teaching for people to succeed in the future. What would I hope we were being taught if I was in school now?

The result was a sort of curriculum of the skills that I believe success will hinge on in the years to come. I'm not going to encourage you to go out and become a coder but instead to focus on problem solving. And I'm not going to try to force you to learn Mandarin Chinese but rather to develop your communication skills. Right now, the need for coders is huge, but in a couple of decades, machines may be coding most of their algorithms themselves and coders' work will consist of different tasks. And in the future, maybe we'll use real-time AI interpreters that provide translations directly into our earbuds from any language wherever we are in the world. This book focuses on the skills that will still retain their value in twenty years. Lifelong learning needs to start with lifelong skills. If a skill receives additional emphasis in the future, it has earned its place in this book.

Today, most people are optimistic that in the future human beings will continue to excel over machines in some areas, but that may turn out to be wishful thinking. Machine sensors are more accurate than our senses, their cognitive resources leave our brains in the dust, and they can work together seamlessly, while each person is different and imperfect. So it is impossible to give any guarantees about specific skills far in the future, but for now we would do well to develop the skills that will continue to differentiate us from machines for the time being. The good news is that what makes us different from computers is also what makes us happy—the skills of the future will give you a meaningful life.

The skills we value are largely determined by the demands of work. The history of work can be distilled down to two transitions: from muscle to head, and from head to heart.

Originally work was very physical, and what people paid for was strength and endurance. But then the Industrial Revolution brought us machines that replaced muscle power. There was no sense in competing with tractors in force delivery or trying to perform tasks faster than machines in factories. Instead of force, we needed intelligence and education, so what was in our brains came to be our primary asset.

Now we are faced with a new transformation. In the Information Revolution, computers are displacing the competences that we recently considered so valuable. There is no point in racing the internet or in trying to find information better than Google. Machines can store more data and retrieve it more precisely that we can, and the human brain doesn't hold a candle to binary systems when it comes to computing power. Our processors are second-rate, so we have to shift our focus to the skills machines lack: the skills of the heart. A machine has no character, no personality, and cannot behave like a human being. The human contribution to work has already shifted once from the muscles to the head, and next it will shift from the head to the heart. Farmers became factory workers, factory workers became knowledge workers, and knowledge workers will become, perhaps, creative problem solvers. The barn was exchanged for the factory, the factory for the office, and the office for . . . well, we'll see!

We've been fighting against machines for centuries and nearly always found that the machines were better, forcing us to move on to different kinds of work. First, we were afraid that machines would steal our work on the farm, and then we were afraid that machines would replace people in the factory, and now we're afraid for people's office jobs.

Digitalization is no different in this sense. Although change is frightening and we may try to resist it, the world will move forward regardless.

Work has always changed, but now the disappearance of old professions and the birth of new ones is happening at an unprecedented rate. The change is familiar, but the speed is new. The danger is that we will pass on obsolete knowledge to the next generation and teach our young people how to succeed in the past. Perhaps our kids aren't spoiled after all. Maybe they just know how to do things we don't appreciate yet. We should understand that in the future, different qualities will receive more attention: now we need the person and the personality in addition to the skills, because a machine doesn't have a personality.

In Silicon Valley, I asked a renowned inventor and futurist what he would study now if he were young. He said somewhat provocatively that the only sensible long-term choices would be philosophy and the arts. Although there are some hot professions now, investments in your own critical thinking skills and character will get you the farthest ahead in the future. So the surest choice will be to trust in the utility of soft skills and the humanities in the work of the future, because they develop the kind of thinking that is difficult for machines.

One of the key questions about the skills of the future is how humans differ from machines. What are the fundamental differences that make humans and machines see problems differently? The answer to this will determine the skills that people should focus on developing and the work that only people will be able to do in the future.

Machines, and here I mean computers and information technology in particular, need data. Machines like simple, well-defined bits of information, so numbers, values, and figures are their favorite foods. If you tell a machine that a glass contains ten blueberries, it will understand you. But if you tell a machine that a glass contains a lot of blueberries, it will be confused. A machine would understand if you told it there were the square root of one hundred blueberries, sixty percent of the volume of the glass of blueberries, or a random integer between nine and eleven of blueberries, but so far it would have no ability to process words that require understanding context or complex interpretation. Machines will continue to develop at tremendous speed in these areas, but ambiguous expressions will still be as difficult for machines as they are sometimes for humans.

And what if I had used an example that involved the words *good* or *evil*? The machine would have been just as confused. Defining good and evil requires a human. We can argue whether blueberries are good or bad or whether the glass is half-full of berries or half-empty. We can tell why there are blueberries in the glass in the first place and talk about how they look as a still life. We can squabble about all of this, but a machine can give us only a numerical value. We are optimists and pessimists, but fortunately machines are neither.

Imagine an ant running across the floor and jumping onto your head. This idea is silly because we know that an ant can't jump onto your head without superpowers. We've seen anthills and we've learned that ants—despite how strong they are—can't jump anywhere near that high.

But what if we gave the same situation to a computer to evaluate? What tools would the machine use to solve the problem? A machine can't remember its childhood or the summers it spent playing in the woods or the first time it encountered an ant. It's also never poked an anthill with a stick. A machine has to know all the numbers, because without them, it can't solve problems. How big is an ant? How long are its legs? What is its muscle mass? How strong is it? How does it jump? How tall is the target? The equation becomes complex, but that is not an overwhelming challenge for a machine. In the end, the machine might come up with an answer that an ant can jump 0.0133295 centimeters but not 183.5 centimeters. A person and a machine come to the same answer but reach the conclusion through different kinds of thinking.

Tasks that require contextual understanding, situational awareness, and interpretation related to culture, history, or social norms are tasks where we humans are superior to machines. We have all the information we've accumulated over our lives, and a machine only has the data that's been given to it. Even if a machine has a million data points and has reviewed more information than any human alive, it will still give its answer as a probability that only a person can interpret as right or wrong, good or bad, a lot or little.

Every skill in this book requires this kind of thinking and contextual interpretation that machines just can't do. The faster technology evolves, the more deeply we need to understand and interpret humanity. Ultimately, technology is only a reflection of us. It makes us strong and gives us influence, but it doesn't change who we are. Technology can't teach us what's important. That is left to us, because it requires interpretation.

We have a habit of improving the things we can measure, but many of the skills of the future are difficult to quantify with any universal accuracy. Both in mathematics and grammar, there are simple right and wrong answers, but how would you define right and wrong related to curiosity or compassion? What would the test look like that would tell us that your moral courage had risen from a C level to a B level on a school grading scale? Can we administer a test and prove that your communication skills are now twelve percent better than last year? In a job interview, if you say that you're honest, persistent, and passionate, you can't show any certificate, test result, or diploma to support your claim. However, these sorts of skills are increasingly necessary in the world of work, even though it's impossible to test them in traditional ways.

There are methods for measuring skills like this (for example, the Berkeley Innovation Index), but they aren't airtight. Like personality tests, they can tell you a lot about your personal qualities, but their results aren't truth with a capital *T*. We're used to learning multiplication tables and drilling irregular verbs into our heads, but we can't memorize something like compassion, so most educational institutions don't include it in the curriculum. We have to go to driving school and pass a test to earn the right to drive a car, but we don't have to undergo any testing to become parents and raise our children for twenty years. In the end, it's all about what we decide to measure and how. Traffic signs and the rules of the road form a coherent system with clear boundaries, but parenthood is more multidimensional. We need to learn to see value in important skills like this despite the fact that they are difficult to measure.

Our age has been characterized by a focus on efficiency, and our goal has been to accomplish more with less. There's nothing wrong with that, because efficiency works really well as long as we know what we want, or as long as the limitations of our planet can handle it. We can optimize and prioritize. However, the future will also challenge this way of thinking. In an uncertain environment, we may not know what we want or what is expected of us. That's why thinking in terms of efficiency won't work anymore.

Now we're being asked to be prepared for multiple different future scenarios, often simultaneously. Because the future is uncertain, our attempts at prediction will inevitably be inefficient, at least in retrospect. We have to get used to this. We know that climate change is real, but we do not know where the next wildfire will break out. We know that the economy will experience another recession, but we don't know where, why, or how. We know that certain events are sure to occur, but we still don't know how to predict them accurately. However, prediction remains important, because even if the final scenario plays out differently than we expect, the exercise of making predictions will still yield valuable by-products. Prediction allows us to react more quickly to changes when they happen. This is future literacy.

In exactly the same way, we should work on developing all of these different future skills, even though some of them are likely to turn out to be more important than others. We know, for example, that creativity is important, but we don't know whether a machine can learn to be creative. We know that perseverance is valuable, but we don't know how that will manifest in everyday life when everything can be predicted using huge masses of data. It's very possible that some of my predictions about the abilities of machines are too conservative. There are already many tasks computers can perform that we would traditionally have thought always require human creativity—for example, analyzing the plots of movies and then making recommendations for a story arc. Maybe in the future a machine will be able to write the sequel to this book!

We can't be sure about the future, which is why a certain amount of self-deprecation is important. I don't know the future, and neither do you, and no one can be perfectly prepared to deal with something that hasn't happened yet. Some of the most respected institutions in the world have been completely off the mark when they've tried to predict what is to come. All we can do is try our best and develop a diverse skill set.

When I was in kindergarten, Petri showed us how the Brazilian football virtuoso Ronaldinho practiced his ball skills. He became a great attacker, who made it into the Champions League, scored amazing goals, and won championships. I saw his success as a simple sequence of events, and that motivated me to practice for hours on end. We bought training cones and built a goal in our backyard, where I would spend hours shooting.

Now I wonder how we can convince children that age to read or attend concerts. Reading will improve your imagination? Attending concerts will help you learn to listen more intently? Both examples are true, but the goals may not feel concrete enough.

We must believe that educating our hearts will bring results, success, and happiness. It's hard to know what you may want to do in the future, but it's even more difficult to say what you can do today to bring that about. This book will help with both.

1

TECHNOLOGY AND THE FUTURE

Technology will change each of our lives in the future more than we can imagine. Is that good or bad?

We are living through what may be the most exciting time in the entire history of the world, because technology is advancing at an accelerating pace and changing our environment faster than ever before. In the future, we will need to know the basics of artificial intelligence, robotics, virtual reality, blockchain, nanotechnology, and synthetic biology in the same way today we understand how to use a computer, what the internet is, and everything a phone can do.

The ultimate purpose of technology is to be better than us or to help us to do things better. There isn't enough strength in our muscles to fly from one continent to another, so we invented airplanes. Our eyes can't see into other galaxies or investigate anything at a cellular level, so we invented the telescope and the microscope. And because our brains can't remember everything at once, we developed a way to store data on computers. In this sense, the human body is very limited: travel across the ocean is possible by boat but not swimming; our eyes can't record the colors of the sun setting over the sea very well, but a camera can; and we can't send that picture to our friend using telepathy, but with the internet, it happens instantaneously. When our skills are superseded by new inventions or we lose our jobs because of innovation, that isn't anything unnatural that we should fight—it's the whole point of technological development. Without this kind of innovation, we still wouldn't have fire, the wheel, or computers.

Technology is a tool, and a neutral tool at that. It is not fundamentally good or bad. The use it is put to defines its morality. A knife can be used for good or evil, just like fire. If fire were invented today, would it be legal even though so much evil can be accomplished with it? For hunter-gatherers, fire was a necessity, so questions like that never occurred to them. Fire only became a threat later when it was misused. Will the same thing happen with artificial intelligence? Even though some technology may appear radical, seen from the future it may be a very natural step forward, even a necessity. New technology has always aroused fear and concern because it deviates from what we're accustomed to. As we evaluate benefits and costs, we must consider the spirit and needs of the age. There was life before fire, but taming fire made everyday life better. We got along without artificial intelligence, but soon it will help us every day—if it isn't already.

The most significant inventions of our day relate to information technology, to things that process information in some way, such as computers, smartphones, and block-chain. Gaining a greater understanding of these innovations can broaden our perspective in new, immensely interesting ways. People need to gain practical experience with how sensors work, how networks are built, and how code is written, to choose only three examples. When we under-stand the basics, our relationship with technology is more positive and it's less likely to feel like magic. Likewise, if we want to understand the logic that underlies information technology and how it can be applied, we need to experi-ment with it. A general awareness of the direction the world is moving in and what megatrends are on the horizon is critical to our success and our ability to form an opinion about developments in society, politics, and technology.

What would happen if we spent a little time every week at school, at work, and with our friends talking about trends and news related to the future and technology? And what if the TV news didn't just cover current events, weather, and sports, but also future news? It's important for us to make talking about the future a part of our daily lives so that we can keep up with technological change. Then the change won't frighten us, it will excite us. Instead of feeling anx-ious, we won't be able to wait!

FORTUNE-TELLERS AND FOLK REMEDIES

There are many challenges in predicting the future. We've traded fortune-tellers for futurists and omens for trend analysis. Although futurology is a science, predicting tech-nological developments is usually easier than predicting people's reactions to it. When technology challenges our old mind-sets, our reactions can be inexplicable.

People predicted that the internet would increase our free time and reduce our amount of work, but instead we live in an increasingly hectic society. Urgent work assign-ments and stress come home with us on our phones and laptops. The goal of social media was to connect people and improve our social lives. It did that, but it also funneled people into peer groups of increasing similarity, and now when we think of social media, the first things that come to mind are confrontation and the undermining of democracy. Globally, unemployment is at its lowest point in decades, but on the other hand, careers are projected to be divided into shorter terms with several employers. In the workplace, we are encouraged to be active on social media, but you can lose your job over a single tweet.

Before, we were more willing to share of ourselves, but nowadays we're more careful about whom we help. We are building our walls higher instead of our tables larger, even though the world has become more connected. What are the future trends we don't yet see? Although our intentions may be good, we can't know what the end result will be. People's reactions to change are difficult to predict, and few are able to anticipate these types of phenomena in time.

Predictions themselves also affect outcomes. If one week before an election someone issues a prediction that one party's support will see a huge rise, many voters may react by switching candidates or parties. If no one had ever given the prediction, the voters wouldn't have changed their minds at the last minute. Predictions are not important in themselves, but they are important in terms of what they cause in us. What the media reports, what's written in books, and what experts say changes our behavior and alters events. That's why predicting the future is difficult. For example, if the media is constantly going on about how artificial intelligence is taking jobs, social media is going to hell in a handbasket, cryptocurrency is replacing real money, or entertainment is shifting to virtual reality, those predictions can influence the final outcome, ironically enough sometimes in the opposite direction.

Technology will also have unknown downsides, many of which we would prefer not to predict. For instance, what will be the long-term effects of the internet and smartphones on social welfare and politics? Big trends also bring about countertrends. Who would have believed at the beginning of the millennium, at the height of the rapture over the Nokia 3310 telephone, that within two decades we would start setting up technology-free zones because we need a break from our phones, if only for a moment? Who would have believed that millions of people would end up suffering from addictions to their phones?

The future is unlikely to turn out the way we imagine it now, and that's why we have to discuss it from different angles.

FRIGHTENING BEFORE, FUNNY AFTER

In the midst of accelerating change, our attitudes, concerns, and laws are the slowest parts of technological progress. Caution is not always a bad thing, but history has taught us that often we can be bolder than we are. Now it feels completely normal for trains to run, airplanes to fly, robots to make goods for us in factories, and pacemakers to be installed in people's bodies to regulate their heartbeats. But these were once radical ideas, and people feared them. For example, in the nineteenth century, the supporters of a movement of textile workers who called themselves the Luddites went so far as to attack factories and destroy machines. Our prejudices often slow the adoption of innovations.

If I told you now that one day a person would marry a machine, that food would be made out of air, and that an artificial intelligence party would join Parliament, your reaction might be cautious, even though the first two have already happened. A man in China built and married his own robot wife in 2017, and scientists in Helsinki created a protein powder using a microbe and carbon dioxide that they extracted from the air. If you snorted at the mention of people being afraid of trains and airplanes, but the idea of an artificial intelligence party made you pull up short, maybe in a couple of decades you'll be laughing at yourself and your current fears. Who knows? In any case, it's clear that the steps we have to take now to adapt to the development of technology may prove to be the most radical ever for the structure of society. And that's usually what faces the most resistance—change to the status quo, not the technology itself.

We're terrible at judging what is normal and what is not. We take for granted all the technology that existed before us, but we are concerned by everything that is to come. Your grandparents were suspicious of things that are common for you, and the advancements that you're suspicious of will be commonplace for your grandchildren. In practice, resistance to change is about defending the radical ideas of the past and not accepting the radical ideas of today.

Imagine a situation where I could push you out of your consciousness by pressing a button. Would you consent to the experiment? This idea may seem unpleasant, because your eyes would go dark, you would lose your sense of control and your sense of time, and you would be absent from your body for a while. However, if I asked you to sleep, that wouldn't scare you at all, even though these ideas are identical. I think it's extremely odd that every sixteen hours or so we lose all control of our bodies and slip into an uncontrollable coma. But we don't give it a second thought! Some people even have hallucinations, which we call dreams. The thought of this would be terrifying if we weren't used to it. We were born into a world where everyone sleeps, so this kind of loss of consciousness every night is completely normal.

We have been born in a period of history where the representation of the time available to us is based on a calendar that divides the year into months, weeks, and days. It's normal for us that a five-day workweek is followed by a two-day weekend. How would this concept of the week have been received five thousand years ago? The people of that time might have asked in amusement why anyone was even considering such a thing, since for them every single day was the same, and no one could change that. Now when we suggest that in the future the work of robots may allow us to move to a three-day workweek, people laugh again. We don't find things strange if we've been exposed to them since we were young, whether we're talking about trains, airplanes, sleeping, the week, an artificial intelligence political party, or backing up our brains online. So maybe it will be totally normal someday to have a computer inside us that we can use to connect our brains to the internet and upload our thoughts to the cloud.

Future generations probably won't give a second thought to the inventions that concern us now. Our job is to make sure that we don't pass on our limited thinking.

IN THE FUTURE, IMAGINATION WILL BE THE SIXTH SENSE

The most important tool in developing technology and predicting the future is imagination. Imagination determines what we consider probable and what we don't. If a future concept is easy for you to imagine, for example, drone taxis, you will predict that thing will become reality. A drone taxi is just a new kind of airplane, after all. But if a concept is difficult for you to imagine, for example, teleportation or a time machine, you will immediately say it's impossible. But how different is teleportation from a 3-D printer? We can now send an object electronically to the other side of the world and print it. New inventions often seem like magic until someone tells you how they work.

The future has often turned out to be more than we could have imagined. We need imagination, but even it has its limits. We have to understand that the limits of our imaginations are not the limits of the world. Future inventions are difficult to explain because they may be beyond our imaginations, or we may not have the words to describe them. Imagine if you had to explain Google to people in the 1970s. How would you have described how it works? Because we didn't have the internet yet, words like *search engine* or *algorithm* wouldn't have been any help. Google would probably have to be something like an "answer machine" or an "answer robot," because it gives answers to any questions you ask. Maybe you could have explained that all the information in the world had been organized in a list and this machine combs through the entire collective understanding of humanity for you in a split second. People would probably have replied that a machine with all the answers was impossible. How would it even work? The very idea would have been considered ridiculous in the 1970s.

Don't let your imagination limit the world. It's hard for us to talk about future inventions without the right terms and concepts, just like Google would have been difficult to explain before the internet. An answer machine should have been irrational, just like teleportation, and just like we consider time travel impossible now. We can't really take time travel seriously now, but maybe even that will be possible one day, in some way or another, thanks to new breakthroughs in physics. As science and technology evolve, we gain a new vocabulary that can help us explain ideas that previously seemed foolish. The future will probably be much more than we can describe or imagine right now. If an idea seems impossible to you, that is only your imagination's interpretation. Even absurd things can be worthwhile. Encourage crazy ideas, and don't be the one who didn't believe in the answer machine.

IS A BEAVER DAM THE SAME THING AS AN AIRPLANE?

It should be obvious to you that a train moves faster than you can run. But you probably don't think that makes trains unnatural. In the future, computers may be smarter than you. That's natural, too, isn't it? In the first example, technology replaced muscle power, and in the latter, brainpower. Isn't that the same thing, though? When a bird builds a nest, an ant assembles an anthill, or a beaver makes a dam, we are seeing bird, ant, and beaver technology. A beaver dam affects the water level in a lake and changes the environment in which other creatures live. Is a beaver dam unnatural, then? The fact that we build technology that allows us to dive deep into the ocean and fly high in the sky but also edit our own genes and talk to machines that are smarter than us does not make any of these things unnatural. It's hard to say where the line is, or whether one exists at all.

Before the Wright brothers' first successful flight, many believed that human flight was impossible. This wasn't just a popular opinion, it was a fundamental, deep-seated belief that flying was contrary to the laws of nature. As late as the late nineteenth century, experts said that a material heavier than air simply could not stay aloft. A similar impossible idea today might be that humans could live forever. Experts would rush to say that this is against the laws of nature, because human cells simply can't do it. The turning point for flight was the realization that something can fly through the air without acting like a bird. Once the idea of flight no longer rested on flapping wings, the chains restricting imagination were cast off. And what if a similar change in thinking someday provides the solution to immortality?

Using airplanes, humans learned to fly, and genetic engineering may help us live longer, even though neither is natural to humans. And what if a machine becomes smarter than us because it thinks in a different way than we do? An airplane doesn't fly like a bird, so why should an artificial intelligence think like a human? Maybe the development of artificial intelligence will make a leap forward when it stops mimicking the human way of thinking or the laws of logic in general.

In the future, you could ask a machine advice about whether you should marry your sweetheart, and it might answer yes. Would you trust the machine's answer even if you didn't understand how it had come to that conclusion? This thought might seem frightening if you were in that situation and didn't understand the machine's operating logic. But a lot of people don't understand how engines work or the physics of flight, and that doesn't stop them from driving cars or flying in planes. So, should you use an algorithm to choose your partner? Even if both you and the computer come to the same conclusion, your thought processes will still have been different. And what if the machine had told you not to get married? Would you have listened? It won't be until machines begin using better methods than humans and we learn to trust them that the breakthrough will happen.

We make decisions with our emotions, whether we're talking about spouses or our opinions about technology. Many technological ideas can arouse strong emotions. We get concerned or afraid, or we think that something inviolable is being threatened. These feelings are natural, but if it's any comfort, I can tell you there's no conspiracy behind any of this. Scientists and engineers have no interest in making the world a worse place. They create solutions that challenge old ways of doing things, which forces us to update our values. When we are forced to consider the questions raised by technology, this helps us find what's most important in life. Instead of using our energy trying to resist the inevitable, let it serve us.

WHO HAS THE POWER TO INFLUENCE TECHNOLOGICAL DEVELOPMENT?

In 1589, Queen Elizabeth I of England heard about a new machine that knitted common wool. When the inventor, William Lee, applied for a royal patent, the queen refused it because the machine would put so many knitters in the kingdom out of work. However, William didn't give up and improved the machine by adding to the number of needles so it could also produce fine silk. Again, the queen denied the patent and expressed her concerns about the consequences of the knitting machine. The queen had a duty to protect her subjects and ensure their livelihood, so she did not approve of the machine.

What do you think of the queen's actions? Do you think she made the right decision, or was she only burying her head in the sand? If the queen had been a futurist, she might have understood that preventing the spread of new ideas is impossible. William Lee's machine is considered one of the first breakthroughs that later culminated in the Industrial Revolution. In retrospect, we can see that the queen should have faced the situation and realized that some forward steps are unavoidable, even if they may be painful. And what if instead of resisting, the queen had aided the spread of these machines? She probably would have become very unpopular with the public and perhaps even been labeled a traitor, but decades later, Great Britain would have enjoyed a technological lead relative to its neighbors. Because of the queen, Lee took his invention out of the country and obtained a patent from France.

We're facing a similar situation now. The impact on society of the rapid development of technology is enormous, and we have to be careful that we don't reject it for the wrong reasons—because right now things happen to be good and there happens to be enough work.

New technology has generally been the product of human curiosity and passion. The goal of technology is not to make people unemployed, but to explore something that hasn't been done yet. When we invented the car, there was nothing in place to support it. No roads, no gas stations, no traffic signs, no infrastructure at all—and not even any buyers because of the high price. We just did it because it was interesting. But it ended up creating all sorts of new jobs: mechanics, engineers, auto body technicians, painters, road workers, taxi drivers, food delivery drivers, and highway patrol officers. If drones, blockchain, or 3-D printers still feel a little superfluous, history has shown that demand for new technologies has often been created after the fact, just like the new jobs. We should invent every interesting thing we can think of even if we don't entirely understand its potential.

Even though technology belongs to everyone, its development is currently driven by too narrow a group of people, especially if you look at gender and age distributions. In the future, we're going to need all of you out there who don't think tech is your thing. You're important because you don't fit the mold. Different people need to be drawn into our discussions about the future so that we can have more perspectives included in the design of new services and products. Remember that it's a privilege to live in an age when information technology is still relatively young and we can have an influence on its development.

We can't talk about the future without technology, and we can't talk about technology without the future. If you want to be a part of building the future, study megatrends, future scenarios, and cutting-edge technology. This is how we can make the world a better place.

FUTURE WORK

- Talk to your friends regularly about future technologies, for example, artificial intelligence.

- Get out there and try every new technology that comes along.

- When something doesn't work, give feedback and help developers make it better.

- Take a critical approach to future predictions and your own fears.

- Remember that the limits of your imagination are not the limits of the world.

- Keep humanity at the heart of everything.

2 CURIOSITY AND EXPERIMENTATION

A person cannot be educated without being curious. The world needs people who ask questions.

The future belongs to the curious. To people who are fascinated by change. We owe every advancement humankind has made to our curiosity, because every breakthrough, big and small, has had behind it the same desire to try new things. Thanks to curiosity, we launched rockets into space and split the atom. Now more new research is being done, more breakthroughs are being made, and more progress is being accomplished than ever before. This is all opening up previously unknown paths and new branches of science. This is the best time in history to be curious. In our constantly changing environment, we shouldn't cocoon ourselves in what we find familiar and secure. Instead, we need to open our minds and start experimenting. And to do this, we need curiosity.

At the heart of curiosity is our strong natural need to learn and understand. Einstein didn't consider himself particularly skilled or talented, just passionately curious. If you don't feel like you have talent either, curiosity will help. Curiosity will get you out trying new things, and trying new things helps you learn. If you ever touched your tongue to a metal pole on a winter day as a child, you know what I'm talking about. You knew it wasn't a good idea, but because you were curious and tried it, you gained firsthand knowledge as your tongue froze.

Curiosity and a willingness to experiment also require courage. Courage to do something whose outcome you can't be sure of. If you don't have the courage to follow your curiosity and experiment in life, you'll miss out on a lot of important lessons. Maybe the purpose of curiosity is to help us find what we want in life. Without curiosity, people act the way they know to act, saying that we've always done it like this, so there's no point changing anything. Invention stops when we lose our interest in trying anything new. The worst thing that can happen to us is that we accept the world as it is without asking why.

When you press the switch, the light turns on, but have you ever considered everything that has to happen for that to be true? In the same way, we get Wi-Fi from a router, water from the faucet, and lightning-fast calculations from a computer. Why? How do they work? The future can be better than this moment only if we are curious. Technology has given more and more of us the opportunity to learn new skills. In the past, someone like the CEO of a business had much better tools than a child born in poverty, but today they both use the same internet and nearly identical devices. Isn't it wonderful that even if you aren't a president, a dictator, or the pope, you get to use the same computers and phones as them?

For most of history, only a small fraction of people have had the opportunity to educate themselves, but now, thanks to the internet, anyone can have the chance to learn regardless of their background. What was once the privilege of the few is now a matter of course for everyone. Now, thanks to their smartphones, first graders have access to more information than the rulers of the past who led entire nations. Even the top advisers to presidents couldn't provide them with information as quickly or as comprehensively as Google does for a seven-year-old.

The information revolution is also a curiosity revolution. Although technology gives us opportunities to learn, it doesn't necessarily make us willing to learn. From studies of human cognition, we know that people don't want to learn things that challenge the worldview they have already internalized. Without curiosity, the internet is just a malign tool that we use only to confirm what we think we've already learned. What we need now is a willingness to experiment so we can learn things that are truly new. Curiosity is like a hunger that grows by eating. The more we learn, the more new there is to learn. And in the future, there will be even more to uncover. Now is the best possible time to be curious—give it a try!

WHAT IF . . . ?

In 986, Bjarni Herjólfsson departed Norway for Greenland to meet his father, and, as is so common in life, the story only got interesting when the original plan went awry. A storm hit, and Bjarni drifted far from his course. Eventually the storm subsided, and land appeared on the horizon, but the crew did not know where they were. Instead of the familiar mountains and glaciers of their intended destination, this place was covered with forest. The crew asked

Bjarni to go ashore and explore, but he didn't want to deviate from the original plan. Bjarni turned course back out to sea and four days later landed in Greenland. Years later, he told the story to a friend, and word began to spread. Leif Erikson heard about what happened and bought Bjarni's ship. Leif then set sail to the land Bjarni had not dared to venture onto, becoming the first European to set foot on the American continent, in modern-day Canada. One thing separated these two men: curiosity. The one who wanted to know went down in history, while the other is a footnote.

Bjarni lacked the courage to try something spontaneous that deviated from his plan. Maybe he was trying to play it safe or was afraid of doing something wrong. This same fear of making mistakes continues to challenge many people today, since it is so deeply ingrained in us in school, where we are usually given instructions about what to do and then told the correct answers. From the very beginning, we are taught to color inside the lines. This seems like a harmless instruction, but it's a good example of how we imperceptibly convey ideas about which courses of action are right and which are wrong. If a child colors a picture chaotically, ignoring the lines, do we scold them for making a mistake? Or do we reward them because they were curious and had the courage to color in their own way?

Historically, curiosity has often been seen as rebellion against authority. Countless stories and legends provide cautionary examples of how curiosity leads to ruin. Icarus did not listen to his father's advice and flew too close to the sun, melted his wings, fell into the sea, and drowned. His curiosity was rewarded with death. The protagonists in horror movies also usually wouldn't end up in trouble if they didn't go into the abandoned mansion alone, but they can never help their curiosity. Curiosity is not always good for us, which is why we've created rules and advice that prevent us from doing stupid things. But we don't have instructions for the future yet. What we need now is experimentation. We need to be curious and courageous so we can create new rules and guidelines to help us manage new technology and everything else the future will bring.

We need to be asking, "What if?" What if there are really five dimensions? What would happen if everyone in the world jumped in the air at the same time? The phrase "I don't know, but let's find out" is one of the most encouraging things to hear. It combines curiosity, experimentation, the unknown, adventure, surprise, and unpredictability. Those few words would have allowed Bjarni to discover Canada and that child to color a masterpiece. However, the phrase has also led to some of us learning that we should not fly too close to the sun. Curiosity can be a curse or a blessing, but every example is united by one thing: curiosity has always led to learning.

HI, I'M PATRIK

I believe that we all have stories we aren't particularly proud of but that have still taught us something significant. The challenge is that sharing such stories often skirts the lines of good taste, humor, and situational awareness. You might be a little ashamed but also smile with contentment when you reflect on the life you've lived.

Don't worry, this isn't going to be a story about a drunken escapade. It all started one day in my middle school Swedish class.

In the ninth grade, we got a new teacher. I happened to sit next to my friend Patrik, and without any specific plan, we decided to play a prank by switching names. The teacher had already started roll call, and soon it was Patrik's turn. I raised my hand and gave a convincing smile. "Here!" For teenagers, little tricks like this are like a shot in the arm. We kept it up all hour, and then the next day and then the next, backed up by the rest of the class. I answered to Patrik's name, and he answered to mine.

We were accountable to each other, for good or ill. If one of us acted out and did something stupid, the other would settle the score, and it wasn't long before things started to spiral out of control. It was liberating to get to do whatever I wanted at someone else's expense, but soon we realized how wrong things were going and decided to do our best in our Swedish lessons in the future. To tell the truth, I don't think I've ever learned as much as I did in that class, since I had peer pressure to motivate me. The requirement of the curriculum that I study Swedish turned into something else entirely. We did all our homework with precision, we helped each other, and sometimes we whispered answers so that when the other person received praise, the reward would end up in our own column due to the name change. To add some spice to the story, the teacher knew that Patrik had attended his first two years of school in Swedish, so he had a better foundation than me. So I really had to work to perform up to that standard. It would have been strange for Patrik to make stupid mistakes on the basics.

Hours turned to weeks, weeks turned to months, and then at some point, as Christmas approached, we realized we were caught in a vicious circle. The more time passed, the more difficult it was becoming to reveal the truth. But on the other hand, everything was going great, and we were learning Swedish while simultaneously amusing the rest of the class. In a sense, our prank had taken a positive turn, and we didn't have any need to change anything. However, we did decide to take our tests with our real names so that when we turned in our papers they would get mixed up in the pile and the teacher wouldn't see which exam belonged to which boy. So we received the grades that corresponded to our skills.

In the spring, attention began to turn to national exams and diplomas. We intended to keep up the charade to the end and solidify our status as legends among the student body. Then reality hit. We realized that at the Spring Festival, when the graduation certificates were handed out, all the teachers would be present, including our Swedish instructor. What would she think when she saw Perttu accept Patrik's diploma? Our amazing prank was about to crash and burn. We started trying to figure out if we would be punished when we were exposed. One classmate's father was a police officer, and through him we learned that lying about your identity at an official event could lead to a criminal record. This hit us like a bucket of ice water. It meant that we had to face our Swedish teacher and tell her our real names as soon as possible. However, it was already April, and we had been lying to her for almost the whole year.

The classroom had never been as electric as on that sunny afternoon. Our classmates were grinning, and the teacher was blissfully unaware that a fraud that had been going on all year was about to be revealed. Ten minutes were left in class when we decided that now was the time.

We stood up from our desks and walked up to the teacher. I said straight out that my name was really Perttu and my friend was Patrik. The teacher couldn't believe her ears. Class was dismissed instantly, and we were sent home.

For the next few days, the school was in an uproar. All of the teachers and students heard about our prank, and the reception was extremely varied. We didn't even know what to think ourselves. We had teachers scowling at us and kids we didn't know giving us high fives. Eventually we were called into the principal's office and instructed to bring with us an explanation of how we managed to pull off the prank and why we did it. A couple of days later, a written warning was delivered to our homes. One more detention and we would be expelled.

This experience taught me that lying is for cowards. To tell the truth and be honest—that's the adventure. Curiosity and an eagerness to experiment are no reason to do anything wrong. We were curious, we experimented, and we learned our lesson. We would behave ourselves for the rest of the school year.

HUNGER GROWS AS YOU EAT AND CURIOSITY AS YOU ACT

In the twentieth century, many people around the world lived in even more impenetrable bubbles than now, because the working class and the bourgeoisie had their own newspapers, neighborhoods, stores, and sports clubs. There are still bubbles, but now they are virtual. Even though at first blush it looks like we're free to choose anything from an endless array of alternatives, we ultimately tend to choose familiar, safe alternatives. We could choose any song on

Spotify or watch any movie on Netflix, but we are less frequently exposed to truly different options than before.

This is poison for curiosity, which depends on new stimuli. Back when we listened to radio, sometimes we heard music we wouldn't have known to look for. And sometimes television channels showed movies we would not have chosen. Once I told an eight-year-old about radio, and she didn't get the point. She wondered why she would want to listen to music that someone else had chosen for her. I tried to explain, but it didn't help. She took it for granted that she could decide for herself what to listen to.

Consider what the most fun and most important experiences of your life have in common. I'd be willing to bet that unpredictability and surprise frequently played a role. Did something you weren't expecting occur? Now that GPS tells us exactly what route to take, we never get lost and stumble across someplace new. Mobile maps tell us where the nearest cafés are, so we don't have to look for them. We have to learn the courage to jump off these prelaid tracks. What if we drove around aimlessly sometimes, chose our movies by rolling dice, or let the radio station decide what we listen to most of the time? Experimentation is partially about making a conscious jump out of your own bubble and adding randomness to life so that not everything is predetermined, optimized, and planned.

For many years, I have consciously tried to be as open as possible to new experiments and experiences. I think that curiosity may be the best incurable disease. This philosophy has led me to some very unexpected places. My life experience up to this point has taught me that you can get through almost any new experience you dare to try if you're willing to make embarrassment your friend. Usually, suffering a lit-tle embarrassment is about as bad as it gets, so try to embrace it. All of my risky experiences have ultimately been reward-ing. I've played the young Jesus at a summer theater, I've sung backup for an artist in a sold-out arena, I've played organ at a hockey game on live TV, and I've accidentally almost shoved my finger right in the mouth of a raccoon dog. Yes, accidentally.

I was walking our dog once in the woods when it started to rain. Luckily there was a shelter nearby that I'd built. When we got there, the dog started sniffing furiously at the crevices in the floor. A strange growling started, but it wasn't coming from my dog. I peered through the chink between two floorboards but didn't see anything but blackness. I was into photography at the time, so I happened to have a camera with me. Turning the flash on, I shoved my hand under the floor and took a picture. However, all I saw on the screen was another board, which blocked my view. I shoved my hand under again, but this time deeper, past that board. I snapped another picture. Now on the screen I saw the raccoon dog, which was looking at the camera from about ten centime-ters away. It had also come to the hut to shelter from the rain. In this story, as in life in general, it wasn't until some-thing unexpected happened that the story got interesting. For Bjarni it was a storm at sea, and for me it was rain. We should be open to unexpected events that change our plans.

But there's no sense being stupid. Once I went on a pho-tography outing to a nearby swamp. It was autumn, and the fall colors were beautiful. I waded through the swamp as quietly as possible, because there were ducks around and I didn't want to disturb them. There was this one duck I wanted to get a close-up of. I sneaked closer, all the while watching through the lens of the camera. Keeping focus on the duck, I zoomed in. I was just a few meters away. Then I heard an enormous bang, and for a fraction of a millisecond I thought that someone had shot me. I've never been so startled in all my life. My knees went limp, and I collapsed to the ground. But quickly I realized I hadn't been hit, so my dramatic fall had been unnecessary.

I'd forgotten that duck hunting season had begun a few days earlier, and I was wearing forest green instead of something bright. You can imagine how fast I ran out of there. I didn't see anyone along the way, but I sang all the way home to make myself known. I can only imagine how silly I looked when that bang went off. But I've never forgotten to check the hunting calendar again. When learning is associated with a feeling or a memory, we usually carry it with us longer. But to learn new things, we must diverge from the familiar.

ASK QUESTIONS THAT CAN RECEIVE SURPRISING ANSWERS

In many societies, curiosity is considered distracting. Asking too many questions may irritate people, and a person can earn a reputation for being difficult if they constantly stick their noses everywhere. We tell children to listen more than they speak and not to interrupt. But curiosity does not create problems—it solves them. We should encourage curiosity, because there is no better company than a curious friend. We shouldn't reject curious people; we should try to create that same curiosity and enthusiasm in ourselves. How can we cultivate curiosity in our daily lives, and how can we succeed in turning curiosity into action? Being interested is not enough. Your curiosity has to show.

Good questions help us get moving. Ask questions that can receive surprising answers. If we ask questions we mostly already know the answers to, we aren't curious. Second, remember that the more things we're involved with, the more we will be exposed to interesting ideas. Good ideas are born out of experimentation and action. Usually, the only breakthroughs that history records are the ones that demonstrate exceptional genius. However, such success requires the courage to try, to ask questions, and to work hard. There's no use brooding over your ideas. Try them out. It's better to get an answer about whether your idea will work, even if that answer is no, than to remain in ignorance. Be curious, ask questions, and try things out.

We like magic tricks because they surprise us. After the trick, we feel a tingling curiosity, because we want to know how the magician did it. If only we could have the same curiosity toward everyday things. In a future based on life-long learning, we will not have the luxury of indifference. If we succeed at developing our curiosity, we will succeed in this changing world.

FUTURE WORK

- Dare to try. Remember that you can survive anything with a little embarrassment.

- Ask what-if questions.

- Never stop wondering. Always ask when you don't know something.

- Talk about the future with children.

- Let randomness surprise you, and be spontaneous. Stop hesitating!

- Don't let anyone discourage you from being curious.

3 CREATIVITY AND IMPROVISATION

Repetitious work can be replaced by machines, but creative processes are difficult to automate, because the end result is unknown.

It connects da Vinci, Shakespeare, Einstein, and Picasso. It's a skill that is more in demand now than perhaps any other. And we all have it: creativity. This is the single most basic need of human nature. Creativity is about play, curiosity, imagination, and having fun. People are at their most creative when they are enjoying themselves.

All of us are creative. We just express it in different ways. In the future, we will be thrust into situations with which we have no previous experience. In the face of new problems, we will need creative people who think in imaginative ways to find solutions. We always need creativity when we begin a process without perfect knowledge of the outcome. If your job is to build a Lego house in the shape of a cube using four pieces, you can imagine the end result down to the last detail. You could make instructions that even a robot could follow. But if the task was to build a Lego mansion, two people would immediately devise different visions of the end result. Any work that requires making choices requires creativity and imagination. In the future, almost all our work will be like this! Repetitious work can be replaced by machines, but creative processes are difficult to automate, because the end result is unknown.

We adults try to be smart, clever, and inventive to demonstrate our competence, but often our goal is to find the right answer, and when it is, our goal is not to be creative. The culture of right and wrong answers we learn in school suppresses independent thought. When we reward the right answer instead of the process, we begin to care only about the final result instead of the method. For the future, we need to unlearn this outcome-oriented approach and the framework of right and wrong answers it entails, because it is poison for creativity. Creativity is improvisation, which doesn't give you time to think about right and wrong. Creativity is play, and play is difficult for a machine, because a machine has no imagination. For a robot, child's play is a utopian dream.

As we age, we usually lose our ability to think creatively the way children do. Children are brash, silly, and hilarious, and they don't start out by classifying ideas as good or bad. Children are excellent prognosticators of the future and great problem solvers, because they haven't become locked into any specific pattern of thought. We should strive to maintain that creativity. The ability to think like a child, without inhibition, is the wellspring of creativity. In the world of algorithms, artificial intelligence, and robotics, we need creativity in addition to logic.

As we tackle the great challenges of the future related to climate change, politics, or education, we will need to rely on our creative instincts. It's impossible to know the result in advance, because the world is always changing. In terms of creativity, it's important to learn to improvise, to make quick decisions, and to treat mistakes like part of the creative process. That's why we need to make creativity a part of everyday teaching and emphasize the importance of imagination among students. Creativity may be the only thing that allows our minds to be analytical and intuitive at the same time. In the future, we will need both precision and mistakes. That is the ideal: balance.

CREATIVITY IS SMALL CHOICES

I believe that every human being is creative at birth, even though some people see themselves as less creative than others. Ultimately, creativity is just the ability to make choices. If you're tasked with making a chair, you have an endless number of alternatives. A chair can have one, two, three, or four legs. You can make it out of wood, metal, or plastic. It can be blue, striped, or partially transparent. Imagining the possibilities isn't hard.

People we admire for their creativity are good at making choices. A flat chair with one leg that is partially transparent and made of metal may not necessarily be the best combination. In terms of ergonomics, a shape that conforms to the human body might be better, and a one-legged chair is not the most stable. Except . . . what if we stretch the chair taller, make the leg round and stable, choose a heavy metal to give it a feeling of quality, and make the seat section transparent—then we have a bar stool! Creativity is ultimately quite simple. It is the ability to make choices and distinguish the most promising ideas from among thousands of possibilities. The old adage that the more options there are, the easier it is to find a good idea still applies. If you invent ten thousand different ideas, you may find one true lightbulb.

In making choices, intuition helps a lot. Intuition is like a personal assistant for the creative person—it helps with routine activities. A person in Silicon Valley who worked closely with Steve Jobs told me they had observed that Steve had developed a unique ability for intuition in decision making. The leaders of large corporations must make many choices every day, and they don't have the option to become deeply informed about every issue. Because of this, they must trust their intuition. Steve Jobs had managed to develop such a subtle intuition that he usually made the right choices. Through many good decisions, the company he led was able to create more successful products than their competitors. Was that because Jobs was a great visionary or because he was a master of small choices?

We need a lot of ideas in order to find the best, but choices are easier to make when there are fewer options. Creativity is a paradox. Small choices are easier to make when resources are limited. When there are two jars of jam on the supermarket shelf, the choice is easier than when there are four different flavors in three different sizes. If all possibilities are open, making decisions becomes burdensome. Creativity is activated when tools, resources, and options are limited. If someone were to simply tell you to make something creative, you might have a hard time getting started, but if they ask you to do something specific, such as making a chair, that gives you a set of preconditions, and beginning is easier. So it's a myth that complete freedom would help us progress. The opposite is true.

Lego blocks are a good example. A basic Lego brick is a very simple object, and there aren't that many ways you can set one on top of another. Overlapping or sideways. That's pretty much it. And this is the great genius of Lego. Bricks with limited possible uses make starting easy but force you to seek out new solutions when you want to build new structures. The leadership at Lego often refers to an example where participants in a group are asked to build a duck with seven pieces. Apparently, they never get two the same. Building with Lego bricks is a highly creative activity, whereas pure freedom does not challenge us to create. The mental block you feel when staring at a blank sheet of paper may make you think you aren't creative, but that's false. Creativity is making small choices with limited resources. And believe me, resources will always be limited! You just have to start.

MISTAKES CAN BE BLESSINGS AND DABBLING A DELIGHT!

Machines have no imagination, but can machines, these miraculous manifestations of logic, still be creative? That depends on how you define creativity. A machine, a robot, or an algorithm can write a poem or compose a song, but it creates its work according to the instructions given to it. It cannot make unintentional mistakes, and it cannot change its mind midstream, which is central to the creative process. A machine can be given an instruction to make random choices or to choose incorrectly, as if violating its own algorithm, but then this is just another action that a human has consciously designed.

Imperfection makes people unique compared to machines. Mistakes have allowed us to expand our thinking and make discoveries we weren't looking for. When I play the piano and my fingers accidentally hit a wrong key, this often sparks a new idea. Without mistakes, all of my melodies would only be products of my own limited imagination. Our imperfection is like a crack in a dungeon cell that allows us to peek through and see what's outside. Through that crack we see outside the box.

Creativity requires that we know how to treat mistakes like part of the creative process and continue despite small bumps in the road. We should accept different ideas instead of fighting them. Genuinely creative people don't care about mistakes. They fill their drawers with songs or poems regardless of how bad they are, because creativity is an activity that demands attention. A creative person enjoys being able to do what they do, and the opinions of others do not detract from their joy.

History has shown that exceptionally creative people have had more bad ideas than their colleagues. Isn't it a strange thought that those visionaries of science and technology who have left us with all these incredible breakthroughs fumbled more than their rivals? This is simply a result of them having done more work. When you have a lot of ideas, numerically, there's plenty of room for bad ones. Picasso created more than twenty thousand works of art, so there were any number of subpar pieces. When Einstein developed the first version of the Theory of Relativity in 1905, he was simultaneously working on five different theories. He published four theories and his dissertation, all in one year. Couldn't he concentrate on one thing at a time? Einstein dropped out of school. He didn't have the skills required to succeed in the job market, and he only managed to get into graduate school thanks to his mathematical skills. Some people thought he was an aberration. Whether we're talking about art or research, many would have advised Picasso or Einstein to focus on one thing and do it well. But would something essential have gone uncreated or undiscovered?

In the United States, I heard from a former CIA agent the story of a leader who began a demanding job in the satellite unit. He worked hard and succeeded in his duties. But one day he was surprised to find himself being fired. He was outraged, because as far as he understood, he hadn't done anything wrong; on the contrary, not a single satellite launch had gone awry during his tenure. The leader asked why he was being tossed out, even though he had done everything impeccably. He was told that he was being fired precisely because he did not make mistakes. He stayed in his comfort zone. Over the years, the Central Intelligence Agency had learned that when a person gives their all, they make mistakes, and the whole agency learns from those mistakes and becomes better. I have no way to verify the truth of this story, but it stuck with me.

It would be reassuring to have a job that you could keep only if you made mistakes. We would have the courage to be creative in an entirely different way if we understood that mistakes are a blessing and dabbling is good for us.

IMPROVISE YOURSELF

Improvisation is the best way to develop creativity, because it involves making quick decisions and accepting mistakes. Like creativity, improvisation requires boundaries, but after that, the road is wide-open. In the future, we will be required to be responsive and to have the ability to react quickly to change. In other words, we will need to make decisions without instructions. How will societies, businesses, or schools improvise in the future?

We can widen our own thinking and practice improvisation with the help of technology. Many people are familiar with brainstorming and concept maps, but there are many other similar exercises—for example, writing feature sets, inventing bad ideas, playing word association or question games, and listing use cases.

In a feature set exercise, the goal is to break apart an idea, a product, or an object and identify all its features. This helps to see the potential of an idea, and all its different attributes and components. Think of a hammer, for example. A hammer's most important parts are the face and the claws, but the hammer has plenty of other features: the grip, head, cheeks, and handle. Could we use those features in certain situations, too? It's a more versatile tool than you think, if you look at it from various angles.

Inventing bad ideas is easy for children but often difficult for adults. The goal is to come up with the worst idea possible—the worse the idea, the better. Kids are exceptionally good at this. If the task were to think up the worst ideas for education, it would be an exceptionally bad idea for a child who gets detention to be sent into orbit in space. Because it is simply an absurdly bad idea. This exercise shakes the dust off our rational thinking and is an excellent way of showing how many ideas are neither good nor bad—they just have different properties. Sending a child out to run instead of launching them into orbit could be a great idea.

A word association game is an exercise where you say the first thing that comes to mind after hearing a given word.

Fly, bird, forest, ant . . . This exercise helps in choosing quickly and moving on.

In the question game, you have to hold a conversation using only questions. This challenges your imagination, because you always have to come up with a new question on the given topic.

Listing use cases is a fun way to break out of context. In this exercise, the idea is to list all the different ways a given object could be used and what commonalities or differences it has with other objects. What's the best way to start developing new ideas? While I was in Silicon Valley, we did an exercise where we divided into groups of five and were assigned to invent as many uses as possible for several objects. We did the exercise three times with three different objects.

First, we were assigned to devise different uses for a fork while one member of the group recorded our ideas. We had one minute. Drumstick, strainer, massager, and so forth. Next, we were given a glass, but we could write down our own ideas. Berry bowl, mosquito trap, magnifying glass, musical instrument, mouse swimming pool, and so on. Now there were more ideas, because we could all write at the same time, and the scribe wasn't slowing us down. With the third object, we were instructed to all work independently. When we listed all the different uses for a pen in silence and then combined all our ideas on the same paper, there were significantly more than during the first two attempts. Hole punch, rolling pin, doorstop, ruler, mixer, and so on.

Sometimes one person's ideas can lead the thinking of a whole group in the same direction, resulting in fewer and less diverse ideas than the participants could have invented if each had worked on their own. This was a good lesson that creativity also demands independent work. Groupthink can end up dominating the process and creating pressure to suggest similar ideas. The spectrum of ideas can be larger if everyone is first allowed to approach the problem themselves and only afterward come together. We need people who dare to think a little differently than the group. It's critical to remember the importance of both stages. Sometimes creative work requires creative methods.

NOT WHAT TOOL YOU USE, BUT HOW YOU USE IT

In the future, both schools and workplaces should be catalysts for creativity. An educational institution or an organization has succeeded if it has increased a student's or an employee's creativity instead of stifling it. Every individual should be more creative at the end of the school or career pipeline than at the beginning. Picasso said that he learned to paint with the technical skill of Raphael in fifteen years but then spent the rest of his life trying to learn how to paint like a child again: freely, creatively, without pressure. What kind of school or job would have helped Picasso in his goal?

Creativity, like courage or empathy, becomes visible only through action. Because of this, it would be important for schools and workplaces to set aside time for creative activities that prioritize the process rather than the end result. In an environment that favors efficiency and control, it can be difficult to let go of utilitarian thinking and surrender to the process. But it's still valuable. Creative expression reaches into parts of human development that are impossible to access any other way. You will not become more creative if you avoid activities where you feel creative. We need to be reminded about this.

Technology has given us a tremendous number of new ways to be creative. The invention of the paintbrush, the typewriter, scissors, and the piano provided new opportunities for creativity. However, it requires judgment to consider whether all tools, such as tablet computers, are good for developing a child's creativity. In one study, reducing the number of toys increased the creativity of child play. It may be that simple toys prompt children to develop a more diverse imagination than apps pumped full of stimuli. We don't know yet which will have better long-term benefits.

It's easier to build new tools than to learn to use the old ones. However, it's possible that in the future small children will apply to music schools by playing tablet music apps. They will clearly be creative and musical, so shouldn't the schools accept them even though the instrument isn't a violin or piano? Once all is said and done, are computers and apps really all that different from brushes or chisels? They are just a new way to connect with creative expression. As long as we feel that creativity can flourish, whether the tools are new or old, all is well. A computer, a piano, or a paintbrush can develop your imagination, and that should be the goal.

Sometimes kick-starting creativity requires getting bored, because many ideas are born when there is no pressure to invent anything. Creativity sometimes requires tedium. In moments of boredom, our minds begin to wander, and our imagination fills in the gaps. At first it feels like time is standing still, but then you forget time, and the hours fly by. In the future, we will need whatever it is that helps us forget the passage of time.

Creativity doesn't come like a stroke of lightning; it comes in whispers. It doesn't look you in the eye; it waits around the corner. Because a creative person is a happy person, it pays to start practicing creativity now.

FUTURE WORK

- Do things that put you in a good mood.

- People are at their most creative when they're having fun!

- If you're stuck, forget right and wrong for a while.

- Remember that mistakes are an essential part of the process.

- Be whimsical and childish every now and then.

- Be open-minded. Eventually you'll find a solution to every problem.

- Don't let ego get in the way. Create because it's fun!

4 PROBLEM SOLVING AND ADAPTABILITY

Problems big and small require an optimistic attitude. A problem can seem impossible until it is solved.

C reativity helps us solve problems, and improvisation helps us adapt. Problem-solving skills have always been central to adaptation, but during times of rapid change they take on even greater importance. The future will bring with it unprecedented challenges, and good ideas will be in high demand. At the heart of problem-solving skills is versatility—versatility to be able to think in different ways, to think through different options, and to see the different sides of a problem.

We should all study a little coding, a little law, and a little art, with some gardening thrown in. Not because we're going to be coders, attorneys, artists, or florists, but because each of these has a very different way of approaching problems and finding solutions. A coder's way of breaking down a problem into smaller parts and a lawyer's precision of interpretation combined with the unconventional thinking of an artist and the aesthetic eye of a florist could give us the tools we need to be more likely to solve the problems of the future. The problems and conflicts of the future will be more complex, which will require the well-rounded thought of multidisciplinary approaches, as well as collaboration between different areas of endeavor.

In a changing world, adaptability has taken on a critical role. Before, the person who got ahead was the one with the best grades and the highest degree, but now it's the person who adapts most quickly. The time it takes before we begin to find that the information and skills we've acquired aren't serving us the way we thought they would has compressed. Memorizing facts is less important now. The floppy disks, paper maps, and Perl programming language that many of us were using just a few years ago are now largely obsolete. Over the next ten years, many applications and devices we now use will likewise become outdated, and we will be required to adapt to even more change and absorb even more new knowledge. Remember that children who begin school in the 2020s won't retire until the 2080s, and maybe even later. Their lives will be like a technological adolescence that never ends. They will have to become future chameleons.

We would do well to try to be as well rounded as possible so we can navigate changing situations in a changing world. In an uncertain future, a well-rounded person will have more opportunities than someone who believes in only one thing. Because work will mainly be problem solving, having a wide range of skills that can be used for solving problems is the best possible investment. If there is only one job left in the future, it will be that of creative problem solver. Who will be the versatile thinkers who solve the problems of the future? And who will be able to adapt best to the new environments we encounter? Hopefully you!

THE MUSICLOCK

I started getting interested in music composition as a teenager, but I quickly encountered the challenges of music theory, especially in classical music. Music theory has never been my favorite subject, but because I had to learn it, I decided to develop a simpler model for myself. I was still so naive. Now, thinking back, my unrealistic expectations were the best possible fuel for solving this centuries-old problem. That is, music theory can look really hard to beginners.

One afternoon I was bored waiting for my mom at the library and started browsing music books. One of the books for adults explained music using grids. The twelve notes were divided into a three-by-four matrix you could use with various patterns to form different scales and chords. I thought this was a fun idea, because I'd never seen music explained without staffs. The layout was off-putting, but the book gave me an idea. Could I do the same thing as the professor who wrote that book and depict music without staffs and notes, but even more simply? If I could explain scales and chords a little more clearly, that would help me compose.

The problem was personal, so I really wanted to find a solution.

Because there are twelve different notes, my solution would need somehow to be based on the number twelve. As I thought about that number, I realized how silly and common it really is. Why does it have its own word: A dozen? Why are there twelves everywhere, like twelve months or twelve hours on the clock? Then I had it! On the musical staff, the notes are in a line, and in that table, they were side by side and up and down, but why couldn't they be arranged in a circle like the hours on a clock face? Has anyone ever arranged the notes in a circle, a spiral, or a wave? I transferred my thoughts about combining musical notes and a clock onto the pages of my notebook and experienced that intoxicating fraction of a second of feeling a little stupid. This just might work. I could put hands on the clock and show chords and scales just like the hands of a clock show the time! And by rotating the hands, the chords could move up or down. Eureka!

I felt confused. The idea worked, but it was so simple that I was almost embarrassed. When my mother came to get me, my trance was broken, but I continued drawing at home. The next day in biology class, I ripped a circle of paper out of my notebook and demonstrated the idea to my classmates, who immediately realized what it meant. I was proud but also a little annoyed, because it had taken me years to learn the same things my friends were understanding instantly before my eyes.

This didn't dampen my enthusiasm, though, and I continued developing the idea all that spring. I made a different version of the Musiclock for guitar and one for rhythms on the drums. For the wavelengths between the notes, I developed a model for easily calculating hertz, and I transformed the intervals into mathematical form on a horizontal and vertical axis. There were so many ideas and so many versions of the Musiclock.

I was excited, but I didn't know what to do next. My goal hadn't been to develop a product, just to solve my own problem. I contacted some professional composers who evaluated the idea and said that it worked. I thought my invention could help other people, too. The public-sector innovation programs replied that I should finish school first, after which I could try to contact them again. It seemed like there were no next steps available for making use of my idea. However, these responses did not affect my enthusiasm for developing the idea. I went on to build a round Musiclock instrument made of xylophone pieces, a disc cut out of cardboard to roll across piano keys, and the beginnings of a digital Musiclock app.

In high school, I heard about some innovation competitions that were looking for ideas developed by young people. I decided to send my idea in, and for the first time I received real feedback, which felt fantastic. The Musiclock won a couple of national innovation competitions, which allowed me to represent Finland in a European Union research competition, where I took home another win. I was invited to share my idea in Brussels, I was invited to the Nobel ceremonies in Stockholm, and I got to attend a big science fair in Los Angeles.

I was eighteen years old when years of dedicated work finally began to receive some recognition. I hadn't developed the Musiclock with these events in mind. Instead, the idea came from the need to solve a personal problem. When you start solving problems that are important to you, you can surprise yourself. It's good to remember than I wasn't the best in my class. I was just persistent. Research has shown that less gifted but more dedicated students see greater success that gifted students who don't set themselves challenging enough goals. Some learn goal seeking as eight-year-olds and some are only forced to do it later.

I learned to be goal-oriented at a relatively young age, and that has helped me more than my innate ability. Maybe it was a lucky fluke that I found my passion and encountered a suitably challenging problem. But central to the process was an appropriate level of naïveté, passion, individuality, challenge, and professional support. Without these I never could have made the progress I did, and I believe that any problem can be solved with these same resources.

THAT'S YOUR PERSPECTIVE

When I received feedback about my work developing the Musiclock from people outside the industry, my idea improved considerably. One of the central dilemmas in problem solving is that we often understand problems really well from our own backgrounds, and that easily makes us blind to other perspectives. We are rooted in the customary practices of our own disciplines, and we often react with indignation when an outsider tries to trespass on our territory. Our expertise often steamrolls outsiders' opinions. Teachers believe they can solve problems related to education, and doctors believe they can solve health-care issues, even though both of these areas are affected by more factors outside those specialties than most of us like to admit.

In a sense, our greatest strengths may also be our greatest weaknesses in problem solving. In the future, we should learn to be open to the perspectives of others, because the greatest insights often come from outside our own fields. The way digital disruption has taken place in various sectors of the economy provides many good examples. The challenger to the television business did not come from within the TV business, it came from internet video services, and the challenger to newspapers did not come from print media at all but from a business model made possible by the internet in which content was entirely ad supported.

No matter what the industry, problems are rarely solved within the bubble.

Different professions see possible solutions in vastly different ways. One of the biggest problems to solve in the current century is climate change. But how? Entrepreneurs believe in their own abilities and think that by making more sustainable products and services they can get millions of consumers to make better choices very quickly. At their best, private companies can be much more agile than governments. But if you ask teachers, they will tell you that everything starts with education. We need to train the rising generation and retrain working-age people so they will understand climate change, its causes, and its consequences. If we ask politicians for the solution, they will point to legislation. They think that regulation is the best way to bring sustainable change to society. Then if you ask tech gurus, they will tell you about the solar cells and electric airplanes that will replace older solutions that burden the climate. Creatives want to increase awareness about climate change through the arts. People are often influenced to change by movies and music. Every profession represents its own way of solving problems, and they are all just as right or wrong.

We have a problem with problem solving if we can't cooperate. The more perspectives that are represented and the more people that are thinking about a problem, the more clearly we will be able to perceive the different aspects of the problem. Only when we understand the biases in our own thinking is it possible to ask for help from others and fill in the remaining gaps. Only when we properly see all the different factors influencing the problem can we begin to consider sustainable solutions.

Diversity is more than a pretty idea. It is the lifeblood of future problem solving. Corporate management teams probably don't need more consultants who attended the same schools as they did. Artists don't necessarily need other artists to advise them. We need cross-pollination so that artists can open up their thinking, processes, and methods to the business world, and the business world can teach artists about strategy, marketing, and customer service. Any group will hit a dead end if all of its members see things from the same perspective. But if the room is full of different viewpoints, it's more likely that someone will get an impulse to move the process forward. I learned this in Silicon Valley when I was surrounded by people of various ages from many fields from all around the world. In that environment, conversation rarely got bogged down in the same old arguments.

In the future, we will need to approach problems simultaneously from as many angles as possible. It will pay to develop skills in creative problem solving and teamwork, because this is what will allow you to participate in solving the problems of the future—including the ones we haven't even encountered yet. Don't accept ready-made solutions as self-evident. Challenge prejudices, including your own. It's better to have problems to solve than solutions to remember.

YOUNG AND COLORFUL, LOUD AND GIGGLY—AN EXPERT!

Historically, skills were primarily passed from older people to younger people. Fathers taught their sons, mothers taught their daughters, and masters taught apprentices. We have accumulated skills and understanding one generation at a time and then passed that on to the following generation. When the world went digital and global through the internet, that millennia-old tradition broke down. A child today cannot ask their grandmother what kind of touch screens she had as a child or what programs she used on the computer.

Because this change has happened so fast, children born in the digital world have learned new customs faster than their parents. This has resulted in an incredibly unique situation in which children and teenagers are actually teaching their parents key skills: for example, how mobile phones or computer programs work. Can you think of any other time in history when such critical competencies were distributed from the bottom up rather than the top down?

In this new situation, we must recognize the special abilities of different ages. Older people have experience, and younger people have vision. There is no shortcut to life experience, and young people can't have it, though a young person who has grown up with smart devices can have something else of value. But think how special it is to belong to the dying generation who lived without the internet and still remembers that time. We're unlikely to ever see a time like that again. They have something special to give, but so do young people.

We need to update our understanding of expertise based on what each person has to give. A seventeen-year-old who is a popular influencer on Instagram or YouTube could well be one of the best social media consultants in the country. A nineteen-year-old could easily join a marketing team, because he knows how best to deliver messages to Gen Z. Even though they're young and have not finished their educations—and they might not look like experts—they can still have important knowledge and skills.

I'm sure I arouse suspicion, too. I'm only in my twenties, and I'm writing a book about the skills we'll need in the future. Plenty of people are certain to think that writing a book like this should require at least a degree in education if not longitudinal research on the subject. However, the hierarchy of information has changed, because information is no longer only available within the walls of specific institutions. Now it is available online anywhere, any time. Globalization and digitalization have given the younger generations a tremendous opportunity to understand the world. They can have a wide range of expertise, even if it doesn't fit into the traditional molds. Our ideas about what competence looks like, sounds like, requires, who has it, and how it is evaluated is changing. Young people can solve problems that older people don't even know exist.

The job search process must also change. Usually the one to get the job has been the one with the best CV and who best fits the position based on their experience. However, in the future the one to get the job will be the one who's ready to learn something new. A worker who is unable to adapt to the way the world is changing will be a poor recruit for a company within a few years, despite a brilliant CV. Job interviews should not look backward but rather ask the applicant to describe what they intend to do in the future and how. The future tells you much more about a person than the past. What people intend is more important than what they remember. What someone aspires to beats what they have achieved. Many pioneering companies have already realized that the most important thing is to look forward, to learn, and to adapt. This puts everyone on the same footing regardless of age.

PROBLEM SOLVING IS IMPORTANT BECAUSE IT IS DIFFICULT

When all is said and done, the ability to solve problems is about planning, and that is something everyone can improve at. Problem-solving skills are also bolstered by many other skills in the curriculum, including creativity and perseverance. In order to improve my own problem solving, I have developed various techniques and habits that I hope will also help you. Here are a few ideas about how you can solve your own problem solving!

On my desk next to my computer, there is always a roll of receipt paper. Receipt paper is great because you can't fit much text on it, so ideas always have to be condensed or written as bullet points. You can pull a shorter or longer piece of paper off the roll, which I think makes it better than Post-it notes. Pieces torn from the roll can easily be grouped depending on the purpose, and notes can also be turned horizontally, for example, to indicate topic. One cheap roll has lasted through years of daily use and has helped me tremendously in my work.

I learned from my mother, who is an English teacher, that you need to process a new foreign word seven or eight times in your mind before it enters your active vocabulary. Once you've read a word, heard it in conversation, seen it in the subtitles of a movie, and so forth, your brain eventually learns it. I think that learning other things works the same way. So I bought a big whiteboard for my room where I can write random notes. The point is that I see those ideas as I'm going to sleep, when I wake up, when I walk by the board, and so forth. In other words, whenever I want to learn or remember something, I write it down where I'll see it. Once I ran into a series of numbers I didn't understand. So I wrote the problem on the board, and I've kept it there for a year. I still haven't figured out how to crack it. But I believe that one of these days when I walk by that whiteboard, I will solve it.

It's important to expose yourself to information that can teach you something new, but even more important to make sure you don't forget your insights. So I also write down all the thoughts I want to keep. I have filled many notebooks with insights and quotations. Filling a notebook takes time, but I always write something each day. You can also use WhatsApp to have conversations with yourself. It's like a personal bathroom wall where you can write your thoughts and ideas. Then you can admire the excellence of your own thoughts when other conversations are less interesting. I find few things as sad as forgetting the details of a good movie, concert, podcast, video, speech, or any other experience. If I feel like I can't make progress on a problem I'm having, the answer often comes from the pages of those notebooks. It's like bottled enthusiasm. If I ever run low, I know where to find more.

Also, no matter what the process, I always try to start working it from the hardest part. This also applies to my plans for the week or day, because it pays to schedule the most challenging tasks for the time when you will have the most energy. When I start a problem from the hardest part, the end becomes easier instead of the other way around.

Problem solving is always challenging, but you can get far with a little planning. Small but functional habits make significant differences in everyday problem solving. Writing things down, whether than means on a scrap of receipt paper, on a whiteboard, or in a notebook, helps me. Other people might benefit from drawing or speaking out loud. The most important thing is to find your own ways of processing information. And sometimes it is also good to try new habits. Maintain an optimistic attitude toward problems and believe that everything can be solved.

FUTURE WORK

- Don't start out thinking about whether something is possible or not. A certain lack of realism is good.

- Surround yourself with people who don't know anything about your specialty.

- Gather opinions from the old and the young, and everyone in between.

- Be versatile! Fill your week with different pastimes.

- Identify your specialties. In which areas are you the best expert in the world?

- Break social bubbles so your thinking doesn't get lazy surrounded by peers.

5 PASSION AND CHARACTER

Machines have no passions or character, and they don't know what they are. Do you know how to explain who you are?

Many of the skills of the future aren't necessarily things that you can pass on in a traditional teacher-student situation. A teacher can teach the multiplication tables and grammar rules and can do their best to convey how interesting the ideas of Plato are, but they can never directly transfer their love of mathematics, their passion for language, or their fire for philosophy to a student. Parents can tell their children what kind of temperament they've had since they were little, but they can't give their children character.

Character and passion are metaskills with no shortcuts to develop. They can be developed only by studying oneself. Can you describe your character and express your passions? These are two important questions that we often don't know how to answer. Part of this may be because we haven't thought about it, so we don't have a ready answer. This question is also difficult because our character and passions are constantly changing. Because our character is our most valuable asset, it also requires active development.

The importance of character will be accentuated in the future, because a machine doesn't have any, although it might appear to. We want coworkers who have a personality. Passion is also important, because it makes us work harder and give our all. I believe that these two attributes create a combination for success in the future. Many people have begun consciously developing their personal brands, and more and more professions are evolving into vocations. If you know what kind of person you are, and you do the kind of work that makes you give your all, you'll be a hard competitor to beat.

Have you ever tried to win against a person with real passion? Good luck! A person who is pursuing their passions is always a step ahead, digging deep, and walking through fire if it comes to that. Think about the things you've done that make you forget the passage of time. How does that flow state feel? When a person is passionate, they release so much energy that you can't even measure it on a productivity curve anymore. They simply have to do more. They want to do more. You can't beat a passionate person. On the other hand, a lack of passion is obvious. How many workers rush to their job every morning without passion? And how much do we lose because of that?

Perhaps character is how you act when no one is looking, and passions are the things you would do even if they were banned. Our world is full of interesting fields, and best of all, the future will bring with it a huge range of new potential passions just for you! The idea of a single passion or a lifelong calling is foreign to me. I believe that we all have many passions. Maybe there are two, maybe three, maybe ten. Right now, the world is wider open than ever for a person with passion. What could we do if our schools made it their number one priority to act as incubators for passion? If we can go through our entire schooling without finding a single passion, then maybe we haven't been exposed to enough opportunities.

In the chapter "Creativity and Improvisation" I asked whether a machine can be creative to the point of writing a poem or a symphony. This example illustrates how the same task can be approached from many different perspectives relative to the skills of the future. Even if a machine writes a poem or composes a symphony, it won't be able to tell us the why of what it created. Motivation comes from character and passion. *I wrote this poem for the person I love. I wrote this song about my childhood.* Other people can identify with these motivations, which has value in itself. What unites us as people is at the heart of the future of work. Experiences like this are what separate us from robots.

We should place value on the individual qualities that make us unique instead of limiting who we really are. If we allowed every child to grow into their unique personality traits and build up their self-esteem, would we only have geniuses? Your character and the entire personal brand that surrounds it will be your greatest asset in the future, because no one else can be you.

BE NATURAL. DON'T GET A CHARISMA BYPASS SURGERY!

I'm happy that I've been given the opportunity to show different sides of myself as I've grown up. When I was little, I was an extremely competitive and self-critical athlete who refused to wear jeans for years because I couldn't run properly in them. As a teenager, I gradually shifted from sports to music. Classical music became my passion, and I let my hair grow out because a teacher at a summer camp said that a cellist needs to have cellist hair. As my hair grew, my style of dress shifted toward flea-market finds. I started wearing ripped jeans that were probably older than I was. I became increasingly bohemian and began wearing bracelets and trolling flea markets in Helsinki.

I was in my first year of high school when I bought a Nepali poncho from a secondhand shop and began wearing it summer and winter instead of a jacket. On the tram, people looked at me like I was an escapee from a Wild West museum, because my big poncho, basically a wool tent, took up two seats and almost reached the ground when I sat down. I started wearing my hair, which reached down to my shoulder blades by that point, in a bun, and this became my new normal. Based on my class photos, you could have thought I was a different person every year.

In my second year of high school, I decided to turn my hair into dreadlocks. If you ever consider getting dreads, I recommend going to a professional. Making them at home took two days, so I had to go to school with only half my head done. I was a little embarrassed, but it was only temporary. When my parents got home, they were surprised to find Tarzan living in their house. They expressed concerns about hygiene, but their worries were unfounded, because I was very conscientious about using pine soap and beeswax to keep my hair clean. If someone had said that this kid with the dreadlocks would soon win Europe's biggest science fair and later end up studying future technology at the NASA Research Park in California, few would have believed it. I probably wouldn't have, either.

All of those stages I've lived through still exist in me. For a while I was a sports nut who won the national triple jump championship and set the Finnish record. But then I was also the boy who walked around in the woods after school wearing a poncho and thinking deep thoughts. I climbed trees and sat on high branches to watch the sunset while listening to folk music. I could make a bird call with my hands and used it to talk to them. And then I was the boy who went to all the science fairs and got called a genius and ended up as a utopian start-up entrepreneur. Personally, I've never felt there was a problem with these overlapping realities, but in some other environment I might have been forced to focus on one passion and to act and look a certain way.

Change is not a bad thing. I'm happy that I haven't stayed exactly the same. Of course, there are some characteristics that have always stuck with me. I still laugh at dumb jokes, I'm easily excitable, and somewhere deep down inside me, I care about the same things I did when I was small. If you don't believe me, then throw a poncho over me and put on some reggae and you'll see what happens.

The personality I have developed through all these different stages is an invaluable asset, and the same is true for everyone. Robots have no childhood, and they can't tell you their life stories, but we can.

MORE IS MORE

None of the stages of my life have gone to waste, because they have all made me more versatile. I believe that we should give all of our personal characteristics equal space. If someone is both a promising coder and a painter, from an employability perspective we might encourage them to focus more on coding than on painting. But I think it's critical for them to paint as much as possible, in addition to coding, because that may end up being the added value they bring as an employee. Painting makes a coder special. We need artists who are good at writing code. We need poets who are excellent data analysts. Even if your day job is writing code or processing and analyzing data, you can see yourself in more ways than one. You can be an artist, too.

We need to seek variety in our personal growth, to support each other through different stages of life and learning, and to develop overlapping, mutually supportive roles. Perttu the entrepreneur is different from Perttu the hippie. Perttu the speaker is different from Perttu the composer or Perttu the little brother. In the future, there will be new roles, and they will require me to continue to refine my self-image. Our self-image isn't either-or, it's both-and. Different roles are not mutually exclusive; they complete us.

Flexibility in one's identity and allowing for different self-images will be a necessity as the world changes. Instead of trying to become something, it would be better to try to *be* something. In the future, we will have new roles that we will need to experience as our own. We may be faced with roles that don't even exist yet. For example, the EU has changed the way I see myself as a European. This is probably quite different from the way my grandparents saw themselves as Europeans forty years ago.

We cannot know what will be required of us in the future, so it will be good to stay receptive and develop ourselves in as many different ways as possible. If we have teaching robots in schools someday, teachers will have to update their self-images. If national borders disappear and the world becomes increasingly integrated, I will have to rethink my Finnishness in a global context. Your self-image, your character, and the roles that combine to form your perspective on the world are constantly changing. Hopefully, none of us will get stuck in the 2020s. Hopefully we will all continue to diversify over time.

THE IDENTITY CRISIS

The world around us is changing faster than our identities. We must give up thinking things like, "Well, *I* could never do *that*." In the future, we will repeatedly have to think about who we are and what our place is in society. It may be that you have to forget your childhood dream job or your current ambitions as the world changes and your fantasies evaporate. A changing environment will put pressure on all of us. We should avoid building our identity too closely around one aspect of ourselves, for example, our current work, because it can leave us feeling adrift when circumstances change.

When I was five years old, I thought I would be an astronaut when I grew up. I loved rockets, space suits, beautiful pictures of space, and the great unknown. Later I dreamed of becoming a lumberjack, a fireman, and a footballer. At the ripe old age of thirteen, I decided that I would become a composer, because I had just visited Mozart's birthplace in Salzburg. I kept my word, and after middle school, my path took me to a music high school and from there to the Sibelius Academy. I even had to postpone my compulsory military service because I was so enamored with fugues, harmony exercises, and etudes. I was on fire as I immersed myself in my dream profession. I did my work and graduated with a degree in composition. But now when people ask me what I am, I never say that I'm a composer. Actually, I don't like defining myself in terms of one profession at all. That's why my answer is different every time, and I usually try to wiggle out of answering.

When we meet new people, we usually use our job titles to introduce ourselves. One person might be a teacher, another a doctor, and a third a police officer. This shows what a big part of our identity our work is. Our professions are an integral part of what kind of person we see ourselves as and what we communicate about ourselves. But in doing this, we have developed a habit of telling people information about ourselves that doesn't actually tell them anything about us. What does a job title ultimately communicate?

In the past it was common for professions and businesses to pass from generation to generation. A bank manager's son was highly likely to become a bank manager, and a child who grew up on a farm was the natural person to inherit that land. Reinventing or changing professions was a much slower process than today. Between the years 980 and 1030, there were no major professional revolutions, while between 1980 and 2030, we have and will continue to see many. At age five, I never could have imagined becoming a mobile app developer, because that job didn't exist yet. Now there are millions of them all over the world. Or professional gamers who get paid big money for playing video games: even twenty years ago, few kids' imaginations were wild enough to dream up that job.

If work life is changing this fast but we continue to define ourselves largely through our jobs, we have a problem. Is it smart to build our identities around something that we might not have in the near future? We're headed for an identity crisis if we are unable to adapt to a changing world and reshape our professional self-images when necessary. Instead of jobs and titles, we should define ourselves in terms of skills and competencies. This requires the ability to see what each person is actually doing in their profession. You have to dig deeper than the title.

Take teachers, for example. A teacher's job is much more than just giving and grading assignments. Even a machine could do that. A teacher's job is fundamentally about communication. Teachers make complex things comprehensible and help students understand them. Another example could be a police officer. The purpose of police work can be summed up in one word: safety. While a teacher needs storytelling skills, character, interpretation skills, compassion, and perseverance, a police officer needs, among other things, communication skills, ethics, problem-solving skills, and patience. If we update our way of talking about ourselves and, instead of using titles, communicate the purpose and nature of our work, we will see which future skills it requires.

If only I had realized at age five that what was important to me was not the profession of astronaut but rather my interest in space, adventure, exploration, science, and the unknown. By focusing on these interests, I could have seen so many other possibilities besides being an astronaut. "What do you want to be when you grow up?" is a question that limits children's thinking. Instead we should ask what they are interested in or what kinds of clothes they would want to work in. If we want to continue asking kids what they want to be when they grow up, we should be asking everyone under the age of sixty, because continuing revolutions in the job market will require answers from all of us.

If you had to describe yourself in one word, what would it be? We need a new vocabulary to give our identity more freedom. Instead of professional titles, we need words that describe actions: enlightener, mediator, campaigner, solver, unifier, collaborator, and so forth. Words like this would reveal more about us and give us an identity that can't be taken away even if a particular profession disappears. For example, teachers could be enlighteners, because their work is the elucidation of ideas. Police officers could be protectors or collaborators who ensure safety in concert with other people. I'm sure that enlighteners will be needed in the future, too, but not necessarily in the classroom. Artificial intelligence, machines, and algorithms may replace assistants and data analysts, but they will have a harder time getting to the level of campaigner, unifier, or mediator, because all of those jobs require empathy and courage.

I like to call myself a colorist. I like being able to add different perspectives to discussions, to add nuance and new shades. Coloring can happen through speaking, writing, or playing music—whatever the medium, I try to bring out the nuances. How could you turn your skills into a title? You may have already come up with an appropriate word to describe your skills, or you may need to ponder it for a long time. In either case, you may feel like you can't completely encapsulate your innermost self this way. But who said you can only express yourself in words?

Our identity is best expressed through doing—for some it's painting, and for others it might be singing or dancing. This removes the filters from our self-expression. It puts us in touch with who we really are. We exist through doing. Maybe the right answer to "Who are you?" is "Let me show you."

DON'T BE A HUMAN BATTERY!

A person who does work without meaning is a human battery. All that comes out of them is what's put into them. If you do only what is asked of you without adding anything of yourself to the process, you're working without character or passion. However, our character is one of our strongest differentiators relative to machines, because personality is difficult to model. When choosing between you and a robot, most people would prefer to work with you, assuming you aren't like a robot.

I'm spontaneous, courageous, and creative. On the other hand, sometimes I'm impatient or rushed, and I have a selective memory, to put it mildly. This combination is unique to me, and no other person or machine is just like me. Unfortunately, people don't usually have a clear view of themselves. The words can be hard to find, and putting names to our good and bad aspects can be difficult. If you can't put an idea into words, it can also be difficult to develop. A new character trait is not easy to create. First, you have to know how to turn a need into a goal, then the goal into will, and will into habit. So to begin, you have to know what you need. Maybe necessity will someday demand that I become more patient, calmer, and less forgetful of important things, like my girlfriend's birthday. Not that I've ever forgotten that...

I believe that our character traits will lead us to our passions if we listen to ourselves. If you still haven't found your passion, the key word is *exposure*. Every experience, person, situation, and memory illuminates our passions a little more. In the past, our exposure was limited by geography, social circles, money, and status. Now, in the age of the internet, we are faced with a global smorgasbord. You can grab as many videos, online courses, and educational apps as you have time to gobble up!

Exposure to new things isn't possible if you don't take the first step yourself. Keep your prejudices in check and try new things. You will have the opportunity to learn, especially when you are prepared to feel a little weird or insecure. Sometimes it's good to be a little nervous. That means you're trying something outside your comfort zone. If passion doesn't come knocking, build a door!

It is also comforting to know that we will all have many new passions in the future. We don't know what we don't know. It may be that virtual reality architect is your thing or quantum computer games knock your socks off, but we haven't had a chance to try those jobs yet. Before the internet, could anyone have talked about their passion for user interface design or search engine optimization? New industries, new jobs, and new possibilities are emerging at a record pace. What will it be like in 2030?

A changing world creates pressures, but it also brings new opportunities and sources of inspiration. Character and passion are a renewable resource. We can change, and there has never been a more opportune time than now. We usually don't admire people for what they know but rather for what they do. We admire them because they have changed something about themselves and also changed the people around them. There is something in these people's character that we respect. Nothing is as magnetic as person with character and passion with whom we can share our work. It radiates. A passionate person is honest. When you get to fulfill your passions, you'll know it.

FUTURE WORK

- Accept all the different stages of your life and be proud of them.

- List at least five different titles for yourself and think about what connects them.

- A machine can't tell its own story, but you can. Don't be a human battery!

- Expose yourself to new things so you can find your new passions.

- Surround yourself with people who are making their dreams come true.

- Listen to yourself. Someone is trying to tell you something.

6 COMMUNICATION AND STORYTELLING

Stories have always been important, but in the future they will be even more important. In a globalized world, stories create connections between different people.

I t would be unbearable to imagine life without any connection to another person. We exist for each other, and no one can survive without human interaction. We are constantly seeking meaning for our own existence and looking to others for support in that pursuit. We're creating the story of our own lives, and we want to be understood. Our character and passions are trying to get out—we just have to know how to communicate them.

With the aid of information technology, we have simultaneously come closer to each other and been pushed farther apart, because we haven't been able to establish true connections through our devices. Interaction skills are constantly changing: our need to experience connection with other people does not change, but in the digital age, we have to relearn the basics. The easier machines and algorithms make communication in the future, the more presence will take on additional meaning. And the more we bring to our interactions as humans, the more value and significance we have relative to machines.

What can you give me that I can't get from the internet? Remembering facts is not valuable in itself, because I can find anything I want using a search engine. As long as I remember to apply source criticism, I can use Google to find accurate information that isn't based on vague memories or false recollections. So, what can I only get from you and not from the internet? First of all, the internet has no body. It can't look me in the eyes or touch my shoulder. A machine lacks all body language. Google has more information than you do, but it speaks without feeling. It isn't excited, it isn't afraid, and it never lays itself on the line. It can't tell the embarrassing stories about its childhood or about the time it surprised itself. Observing emotions and responding to them deepens connections between people. We can be considerate of each other even without words.

In the information age, we are measured using information yardsticks—in our work, we are only as valuable as the information we have gained, for example, through our education. But we have to understand that not all information can be captured by letters and numbers. Information also includes manners, body language, feelings, time management, tone of voice, and silence. The communication of the future will require developing all of these. Information technology is pushing us to refine our communication skills. A machine can write and talk and even give a presentation and a forced smile. Now more is being required of you than that!

In the past, few people were trained as salespeople, marketers, or storytellers, but things are changing. That's a positive step, because these skills will gain even greater currency in the future. The courage and ability to present ideas to audiences and to speak on behalf of things that are important to us in front of people will serve us throughout our lives. And this skill is something you can and should practice. If all of us gave at least two planned, rehearsed speeches every year, we would be much more confident in communicating about issues that matter to us.

In my life, the skill that has had the most positive impact has been the ability to publicly communicate my ideas. I've learned to convey my ideas better and to help others to understand and get excited about them, first by describing my own inventions and later by giving lectures to audiences. Storytelling and communication need to be taught, because even the world's most brilliant ideas will go unexploited if no one knows how to explain them. Solving the great problems of the future will be difficult if we're talking past each other. It's impossible to find solutions if we don't even know how to put the problem into words. We can either learn how to create connections and build bridges, or we will constantly misunderstand each other. You can usually tell the quality of communication by how well we're understood. If someone doesn't understand you, the fault may be in your words.

BODY LANGUAGE DOESN'T COME OUT OF YOUR MOUTH

Throughout history, we have always developed increasingly versatile and complex tools to support communication. Thousands of years ago, pointing fingers and grunting was the same thing as liking on Facebook and retweeting on Twitter today. We're doing the same thing with technology, just in a different way.

In the early twentieth century, people received information from their parents and teachers, along with newspapers or textbooks. In Finland, we gained the opportunity to listen to the radio in the 1920s and to watch television in the late 1950s. New communication platforms are constantly emerging. There are voice messages, blogs, videos, apps, snaps, pictures, stories, emojis . . . and every platform has its own rules and norms. You can't compare a voice mail to talking on the phone, on a podcast, or on the radio. It would be silly to post Instagram photos as TikTok videos, let alone going to Facebook to delete your photos the day after posting them like Snapchat does. The same comment on Tinder or YouTube can mean two vastly different things.

Before, you had to know your recipient's contact information and wait for a letter to arrive, but now you can send messages instantly to people you don't know. Before, a phone was only a tool for contacting people, but now it is an extension of your personality. We live in a multimedia age, and due to new tools, communication has taken on new nuances.

Messages need context to be understood. Perhaps you've noticed this if you've ever tried to tell the same joke in several different places. It doesn't always work! The challenge with these new digital platforms is that they obscure context, leaving more and more of a message up to interpretation. We've ended up in a situation where we can tear our hair out trying to understand a cryptic text message or a strange Facebook post, or spend prime time on TV speculating about single tweets. Because all human communication is deficient, we are forced to try to interpret incomplete and fragmented information. And when we have conversations digitally, without body language, tone of voice, or expressions to guide us, it is impossible for us to understand nuances in opinions. And then we get into flame wars. When username argumentdestroyer latches onto one sentence in the middle of a long message from another poster, everyone else is mostly confused.

In the future, we must actively invest in the quality of our conversations. Sometimes that may mean abstaining, but mostly it means understanding context, noticing when it is lacking, and avoiding cheap tricks. So often we prefer to criticize the author's handwriting rather than reading what the text is trying to say.

We all have different sensors, and we communicate through individual transmitters and receivers. No matter how clear a signal I think I'm sending, the other person's sensor settings on that day might be completely different, depending on their mood or what happened during the preceding week. So they might say they understand me but actually interpret my message very differently than I intend.

There's always a risk of miscommunication in interpersonal communication. When we comment on a conversation and add an emoji at the end, we can only hope that the other person understands it the way we want. A good conversation doesn't make itself. It requires effort. However, this is a skill we can develop.

HOW DO YOU TALK TO A MACHINE?

There are two kinds of relationships: me-you and me-it. I believe that in the future, a third kind of relationship will emerge—me-machine, which falls between the two already mentioned. It is not a relationship to a mechanical machine, because it involves intelligence, but the other half of the relationship is also not a completely reactive human being, either. Instead, it is a sort of intermediate form. This relationship is an example of a new kind of communication that will create a need for new products, services, knowledge, and skills.

How is it appropriate to talk to a machine? At least communicating with machines will get easier in the future. Thanks to artificial intelligence, you will no longer have to speak to a machine slowly and clearly, like you're teaching it to talk; instead, in the future, machines will be able to understand even if you speak with an accent. And what sort of relationship will form between you and your AI friend? Perhaps in the future we will even have a fourth relationship, machine-machine. In the future, every person may have a digital assistant who handles day-to-day tasks with other, similar digital assistants.

Just as we adjust how we speak to children versus adults, in the future we may need to know how to talk to machines in a different way. You can't talk to a child about stock values or world politics using difficult words because it requires understanding of the terminology and multidisciplinary interpretation. In contrast, you can't talk to a machine about unicorns and gnomes doing battle in the forest outside the preschool because that requires imagination and abstract thought. We must learn to speak intelligibly whether the listener is a human (a child or an adult) or a machine (intelligent or less intelligent). The ability to communicate the same thing to different receivers is valuable. Communication is a balance between the abstract and the concrete, the imaginary and the pragmatic.

Understanding ideas at an appropriate level of abstraction is easy for humans. If you say something too concretely, it's boring, and if you come from too high a level, it doesn't feel relevant. The challenge of communication is that people have different perceptions of abstractness and concreteness. Sometimes you have to explain things to adults like you're talking to a child, and at other times you might find yourself talking to a child far too simply, basically talking nonsense. Striking the right balance is extremely important.

Take the heart, for example. At the concrete level, we could show a person a picture of a heart—a wet, red blob full of a million details. At an abstract level, the heart could just be a red circle, just a shape and a color. The best solutions, the ones we remember, combine both. All around the world, people use a symbol with two symmetrical, curved halves, usually red but not always, to indicate a heart. It is both concrete and abstract at the same time. It's easy for people to adopt this symbol, and that's why it gets drawn in the margins of so many notebooks and added to so many Instagram stories.

The same thing goes for storytelling and communication. As we communicate to machines and through machines in the future, we will need the skill of expressing ourselves in the best possible way given the context. Machines are good at understanding the facts of research studies, but people remember better when there is a story attached. We need to know how to talk to machines in their language and to tell people stories that stick in their memories.

THAT TIME I MET A HUNDRED OF MYSELF

The power of stories is incredible. They can make us do things we would never do if they were not part of a larger narrative. One example of this is the gathering of the Perttus in Pertunmaa.

When I was nine years old, a strange letter arrived in our mailbox. Every person named Perttu was being invited to Pertunmaa, a small town in south-central Finland whose name literally means "Perttu's land," to break a Guinness World Record. So, our whole family packed up and headed for Pertunmaa, and I ended up in a big room with hundreds of other Perttus. There were tiny babies, grandfathers, and everything in between. Wherever I looked, all I saw was people with my same name. It was a funny feeling, like a tribal gathering. A moment earlier there had been a long line at the entrance, because official inspectors had asked everyone to prove their names with their passports. It felt good when they let me through. I was the genuine article!

Why would anyone ever drive halfway across Finland just to stand in a sweaty gymnasium for a few minutes surrounded by hundreds of strangers? Breaking the record probably wasn't the primary motivation of everyone who arrived, and I don't actually know if the record was broken or ever certified. But I can be proud that all us Perttus who gathered in Pertunmaa beat the Shirleys who gathered in Alice Springs in Australia by 294 to 122. And we had a lot of fun. We went because there was a story, and the story became an experience. We made the story true.

Storytelling is intimately linked to culture and its development. We live in a globalized world where more than half of the population is online, resulting in a blurring of cultural boundaries and geography. This development has given rise to a countertrend, because now small, local cultures have become interesting. For example, as a counterbalance to popular culture, mainstream media, the entertainment industry, and Hollywood, Finnish culture and language are becoming more valuable and special. The question of who we are and what our background is will not disappear in a globalized world. Quite the opposite. My visit to Pertunmaa with all of my namesakes taught me that the beauty and small scale of localness will always beat globalness.

We need to learn to tell stories that connect people. The stunt in Pertunmaa was about a record number of people with the same name, but it also could have been nice if a few Perttis had joined us. Because only stories that bring everyone together bring important things to pass. Stories about justice have helped us move away from child labor, slavery, and racism. Tales of success have encouraged people to try their best, and fairy tales about love have made us all see more good in our neighbors. Now we are creating a story about how we can stop climate change. We need protagonists, role models, and archetypes. Without a story and emotion, people won't act.

Stories are how we pass wisdom on to children—and older people. They have always been important to people, but in the future they will be even more important, because in a multicultural world, stories create connections between the most disparate people . . . even if the only thing they have in common is their first name.

NOTICE THE THINGS IN OTHER PEOPLE THAT A CAMERA OR MICROPHONE CAN'T

We need to focus more on communication and storytelling because the quality of our lives is only as good or bad as the quality of our communication. Any person who understands context, i.e., the frameworks of communication, will be a master communicator in the future. They will be able to utilize various platforms to be understood and to avoid pointless conflict. It's a different thing to connect face-to-face than on Snapchat, and a different thing to send a text message than a photo on Instagram. Each platform requires unique communication skills and methods of interpretation.

Because every situation is different, there are no perfect sentences that you can always say. There is only presence. Perhaps the fundamental purpose of communication is to teach us to listen to what isn't said aloud and to read the messages that aren't written. Anyone who can understand these messages will see their interactions deepen. If I tell a friend that an artist I like just released a new album, and it's really great, I'm not just talking about the music. The implication of my message is that the album is important to me, and I want to share it with you. If my friend comments that the album art is silly or the singer's breathing is annoying, I may be left feeling that they didn't understand me. I shouldn't have said anything, I may think. But if they realize that this is something important to me, they'll know to take my feelings into consideration.

In the future, skills like this will be invaluable. How can we take into account needs that we don't know how to express directly? A machine's sensors can't measure what only a human can experience. For machines, unspoken messages and subtle gestures are easily missed. They're understandably difficult for them, as they can be for humans. However, we humans have more potential for learning.

The future will require better communication, not conflict, misunderstanding, and provocation. The ability to formulate things appropriately and get people's attention without incendiary opinions, generalizations, and polarizing examples will be valuable in the future. In a world where we are faced with endless options, we must learn to be present. If communication is a difficult skill for humans, then it will also be difficult for machines—and that is exactly why we need to improve it.

FUTURE WORK

- Tell stories that unite people. Be proud of your roots.

- Listen to what others have to say. Keep in mind whom you're talking to.

- Even when your message is on a screen, imagine the other person standing in front of you.

- Don't be provoked by incomplete information. Put off getting irritated.

- Get to know the different communication apps, and learn how to use them.

- Consider what digital messages are missing.

7 CRITICAL THINKING AND INTERPRETATION

The richness of life exists in the possibility of interpreting the same event in different ways. A complex world requires versatile thinkers.

Critical thinking helps us make decisions. At its best, critical thinking is an exciting exploration, a striving to get beyond the self-evident in our thoughts. Without critical thinking, we are locked into our own perceptions, which are not always accurate. Above all, critical thinking is about asking questions, and many of the curriculum skills connect to it. Critical thinking requires creativity, adaptability, curiosity, and reflection. In the world of the Information Revolution, we have to learn to evaluate the accuracy of information and its usefulness depending on context.

The ability to think critically will only become more pronounced in the future, because we will constantly be forced to navigate huge amounts of knowledge, and this flood of information shows no sign of abating. If our critical thinking becomes lazy, we will end up thinking in a certain way even though we don't know why. We will become more susceptible to believing fake news, and clickbait will conquer us. Critical thinking and media literacy are like civic duties that benefit you first and foremost. The internet gave us a means to make our voices heard and influence public issues. It is a wonderful thing for democracy, but it also has its drawbacks. The information that can now reach such enormous audiences hasn't been checked or corrected to reflect the facts. We need to be able to recognize where the line between fact and fiction runs. What is belief, what is knowledge, what is argument, and what is anecdote?

The goal of internet services is not to educate us, it is to satisfy us. Google is not designed to teach us—it is designed to give us what we're looking for. YouTube's algorithms give us recommendations for more of the same content, not opposing viewpoints. On Facebook, our news feed consists of posts that generate reactions, even if the facts presented are false. Opinion-based content receives more visibility than impartial content. Algorithms determine what you should see. But responsibility rests with the recipient, the critical thinker. False claims gain momentum almost imperceptibly on the internet.

At its best, critical thinking strengthens self-esteem, improves language and presentation skills, encourages innovations, and helps us make better choices every day. Interpreting information leads us to develop our listening skills and situational awareness, as well as to consider cultural, historical, and social factors. We need critical thinking and interpretation more than ever now, because only critical thinkers will be able to face our uncertain future, and only wise interpreters will be able to understand the past.

THE QUESTION REVOLUTION

Critical thinking is fundamentally about the ability to ask the best possible questions. We're used to asking questions that have the right and wrong answers, and our entire education system is based on this. Now we need a question revolution.

The internet makes finding facts easy, so memorization has lost its relevance. We've all spent years cramming our heads full of information, despite the fact that the ability to recall those details quickly from memory no longer gives us much added value. Of course, there is pleasure in remembering the Ionic, Doric, and Corinthian columns of ancient Greece! Wait, was that how it went . . . ? The point is that anyone can find this same information in seconds using Google. This means that we need to start asking different questions.

We need fewer one-answer questions (what, where, who) and more questions that have many answers (how, why, and for what purpose). Using Google, it's easy to find answers to the former types of questions, but answers for the latter require perspective, opinion, and interpretation. In the future, interpretation will be more valuable than remembering. Simultaneously, we will be freed from the pressure of right and wrong answers.

There is only one correct answer to the question, "What is the capital of the United States?" If a child answers wrong, they feel a sense of incompetence, perhaps even shame. However, if we ask what the most *important* city is in the United States, the answer could be any city, as long as you can justify your response. You could say Los Angeles, because it's well-known around the world, or New York, pointing to its importance to the economy. You could also reasonably say Silicon Valley as a whole, because so much new technology has been developed there, or Washington, DC, because it's the center of national politics. You can discover the capital of the United States by googling, but forming an opinion and defending it requires thought, so the phrasing of the question challenges us to greater critical thinking and interpretation.

Because the question of the most important city in the United States can be answered from an infinite number of perspectives, each different answer would teach the class more about American cities than simply interrogating children about the capital. Even the teacher can learn when children are given the opportunity to respond critically and not just to give an answer. Imagine this approach being applied to different classroom subjects.

The things that are worth memorizing are constantly changing. We can find answers from Google, but we will receive richer information from people. Critical thinking is based on the right kind of questions, so it's important to pay attention to how questions are phrased. Questions are more valuable and often more difficult to form than answers.

Open-ended questions provide an opportunity to answer in an in-depth way, so it pays to start with a question word rather than a verb. Notice the difference: "Did you study today?" versus "What did you do today?" An answer to a question that starts with a question word provides more information.

The saddest thing is to ask something when we already have an answer ready. Then we're controlling, not conversing. Our own attitudes can very easily color our questions if we don't know how to ask them the right way. And if we allow this to happen, questions can lead to caricatures, black-and-white thinking, confrontation, and stereotypes. To make breakthroughs, we have to ask better questions.

READING IS TWENTIETH CENTURY; INTERPRETATION IS TWENTY-FIRST CENTURY

Before the internet, the value of a newspaper was that it conveyed information. The same was true for books. But because of the internet, this is no longer the case, since anyone can pass on information. Instead, the value of newspapers and books has become trustworthiness. A story in a newspaper was written by a trained journalist and has gone through an editorial process, so you can trust it more than a blog post online. For the same reason, this book is appearing through traditional channels instead of as a PDF on my website or through self-publishing, because the publishing process adds value. Even if the end result looks the same, people are paying for something different. Before, people paid for information, but now they pay for the process, which adds credibility.

As a result of the internet, we are forced to treat everything we read critically, because we're being offered so much free, unprocessed information. Before the internet, there was not the same need to doubt every piece of information the way there is now, because there was usually a publisher or editor standing behind each news story being published. So it's no wonder that research is showing that the people most likely to believe incorrect information on social media are those over age sixty, who have more trouble spotting fake news and trolls. Even when young people believe fake news, they share it less than their parents. Even so, accepting incorrect information online can happen easily to anyone.

In addition to needing to be able to assess the reliability of information, we need to internalize the fact that it's possible to receive information in many different ways. Newspapers and books have been joined by videos and podcasts, among other things. Even as reading declines, people gather more and more information by watching and listening. Should the concept of literacy be expanded? Should we begin focusing on a broader concept of critical interpretation, because there are so many ways of getting information? In the future, interpretation could include many different kinds of literacy, such as the ability to read someone's body language, read a game like soccer or chess, or utilize systems thinking in order to understand and solve a problem. In order for us to understand our complex world in the future, it's essential for us to be able to interpret information regardless of the format.

YOU DON'T HAVE TO INTERPRET HONEST PEOPLE

I've made some rash New Year's resolutions over the past few years. In 2017, I committed to putting myself outside my comfort zone more often. If I had doubts about trying something, I definitely had to do it. In 2018, I actively strove to become a better listener. In 2019, I tried to improve my situational awareness and be cognizant of the mood during any given situation or event. For example, I wanted to understand the energy in a room when I entered it. I believe that a person who is able to recognize the prevailing mood and turn it toward one where other people feel comfortable will be sought-after company.

My 2017 resolution put me into many situations I never would have experienced otherwise. In the summer, I went to Los Angeles on my own and lived there for nearly three months. One August afternoon, I was lying on the beach in Santa Monica scrolling Facebook and happened across an event that caught my attention. Radical Honesty. The event was near where I was, and it was due to start in a little over half an hour, so I didn't have time to hesitate. It would be a new experience, and that was what I was looking for, so I jumped on my bike and started pedaling.

After making it just in time, I stepped into a room where eight people were just sitting down in chairs arranged in a circle. I greeted the organizer and chose my seat in the circle. The group was colorful, to say the least. I couldn't help thinking of the AA meetings I'd seen in American movies, because the setup was remarkably similar. I said my name and how I had ended up there. I learned that radical honesty is a philosophy founded by a certain psychologist, and that there were meetings and trainings being held all over the place all the time. This wasn't just a onetime event.

As a group, we started talking about what honesty meant to each of us. The members of the group believed that we should be radically honest in everything we do and say. Often, we edit or embellish events depending on who we're talking to. We make little concessions to the story because we're thinking of what's best for the other person and don't want to be brutally honest. We try to shield people from being offended, and we think we're doing them a favor.

However, there is a dilemma here. What does it say about us that we don't tell the whole truth, but instead our own version or interpretation? Doesn't that mean we think the other person is incapable of handling the truth? This observation made me think: Is honesty so hard for us that we have to sell our own interpretation to other people? What prevents us from telling the whole truth? Honesty has caused many conflicts, but still. Would radical honesty be fairer? It felt silly that I had come all the way to California to learn this very Finnish skill of speaking directly.

In the next exercise, the purpose was to focus our attention on interpretation. The idea was to make visible how different it is to notice something rather than to imagine it. Because we often interpret things incorrectly. If we notice that someone is wearing a baseball cap backward, we may imagine that they're some sort of tough guy, or if we see someone standing with their hands on their hips, we might imagine they're having a bad day. However, both are merely interpretations, which are often wrong. For some people, the baseball cap will only mean that the person is concerned about burning their neck on a sunny day. Hands on hips may be a sign of a bad day, but that person could also just be focused or meditating. Contrary to what we imagined, they might be in a very good mood.

We need to spend more time asking questions and listening, and less time imagining. What another person says will tell us more than what we imagine about them. Stereotypes are not always wrong, but they are always imperfect. It's actually freeing when you don't need to form prejudices. You can save the brain capacity you were using for speculation and use it on something more useful. In the future, we will need the ability to interpret, but we also need to learn not to interpret too much.

I DON'T KNOW WHAT I DON'T KNOW

The richness of life is that we have the possibility of interpreting the same event in various ways. For example, science and art approach problems differently, but that doesn't make either method less valuable. That's why in previous chapters I've recommended that research types do art sometimes and artist types do some science—to find new ways of interpreting problems.

Natural science seeks to summarize complex subjects in simple propositions or expressions, such as $E=mc^2$, which are universally applicable. A certain interpretation of a phenomenon will exist until the theory is overturned or supplemented by a new interpretation in accordance with the philosophy of science. Art works the opposite way. Each individual work of art gives rise to an infinite number of different interpretations, which are all just as correct. As many alternative truths exist as people experiencing the work. It would be horrible if we had the objective truth of Beethoven's "Moonlight Sonata" or Tchaikovsky's *The Nutcracker*. Everyone's interpretation is unique, and that is the splendor of art.

Science shrinks, art expands—and both are beautiful. The same phenomena can be interpreted in different ways without researchers' perspectives steamrolling artists' interpretations or vice versa. However, what science and the arts have in common is that both result in small increases to our knowledge, while our knowledge of what we do not know increases significantly. And thus the study of the universe goes on, endlessly. Each answer leads to more new questions.

As we meet the great challenges of the future, for example in politics and economics, we must approach them not only from the perspectives of art and science but also culture and history. Every perspective is necessary. Whenever an issue is raised in the media, consider the method of interpretation. Every thought, solution, and model is a product of its time and an interpretation of one sort or another. In the future, we must have the ability to interpret old solutions in order to know how to think about new ones. Critical thinking is required to bring old, dusty interpretations into the light of day.

As we analyze politics, the media, or school curricula, we must understand the tradition from which the original ideas arose. What was the need that current practice was originally developed to meet? For example, democracy in ancient Greece, where it was first developed, was created in response to the ideals of an ancient society, and it worked quite differently than it does today—by requiring the participation of free male citizens and excluding everyone else. Democracy needed to be updated as society progressed. Traditions are valuable and have become traditions for a reason, but they may also inhibit our thinking. In the future, we will need science, i.e., critical thinking, and art, i.e., interpretation, as well as tradition and the courage to question tradition.

No matter what time of year you're reading this, make a New Year's resolution for yourself. Think critically so you can interpret the world around you. Then interpret less, so you can think critically again.

FUTURE WORK

- Ask questions that can't be answered by googling.

- Believe people who ask more than they answer.

- Challenge your own thinking and let others challenge yours.

- Don't waste your energy on speculation and over-interpretation.

- Question, challenge, and search for reliable sources.

- Consider how someone else might interpret the same event.

8 ENTREPRENEURSHIP AND TEAMWORK

Entrepreneurship is responsibility, ownership, and self-management. In the future, we will need more of an entrepreneurial attitude.

In the future we will all get to be entrepreneurs to some degree or another. I want us to think about entrepreneurship more broadly than income and business licenses. For me, entrepreneurship is a way of thinking that first identifies a problem, then creates a vision to solve it, and then executes the plan, alone or with a team, whether large or small. In the future, work will require initiative and the ability to collaborate. The good news is that we're actually all entrepreneurs already. All we have to do is strengthen our entrepreneurial spirit.

Entrepreneurship is much older than we normally think, and much more deeply rooted in us that we might realize. Before the invention of money, we were all entrepreneurs, although no one talked about it that way. We traded our knowledge and skills to meet others' needs and vice versa. What we count as entrepreneurship is a line drawn in the water. Even though Mozart was called a composer, was he also an entrepreneur? The process might have included music composition, recruiting players, reserving a concert hall, selling tickets, and payments to the musicians, after which Mozart could have taken his profits and then done it all again. The product was a symphony, the customers were the listeners, and the business partners were the royal courts and orchestras. Fundamentally, they identified a problem, put together a team, came up with a vision, and executed their solution. There probably wasn't any Mozart Incorporated, but his operation was a business.

Our market economy has led us to define entrepreneurship in terms of business, but in the future, we will need to expand this definition. If you were asked to name some of the great people who have changed the world in our age, what names might you mention? Maybe Bill Gates, Steve Jobs, or Mark Zuckerberg? If I asked you the same question but about history, what would you say then? Maybe Socrates, Leonardo da Vinci, Einstein? Notice that the former are entrepreneurs but the latter are philosophers, artists, or scientists. Even though historical figures didn't issue stock through incorporated business entities, that doesn't mean they were any less significant. They all had the entrepreneurial spirit because they created something significant. Whether you own a business in the future or not, there will still be an entrepreneur inside you.

In the future, many people will be fighting for the same jobs. Entrepreneurship is emphasized in situations where supply is abundant, because that forces you to work hard to be the one chosen from all the options. Right now, just a little over half of the world's population is online, but what will happen when we get the last few billion people logged on? We could be as few as ten years away from that. This would be a tremendous development in terms of global trade and labor, but it would also mean that we would have a huge number of new competitors and workers. They might be able to offer the same work as you, maybe cheaper, faster, and remotely. As world education levels surge, there will be an increasing number of highly educated people even in developing countries in the future. In an environment like that, an entrepreneurial attitude is paramount, because you and I will have to find an appropriate job, sell our skills, seek opportunities, and generate satisfied customers.

Entrepreneurship and teamwork must be taught, because in the future work will become more fragmented. It may be that companies want to hold on to their employees and that they will succeed in retraining them for new tasks as time passes, but updating skills even in this way requires an entrepreneurial spirit. Careers consisting of decades in the same job, with the same employer, or even in the same industry, are not very realistic anymore. Navigating a shifting job market will increasingly become an individual responsibility. In this case, responsibility will also bring us the freedom to mark our own paths. As an entrepreneur, you are free to create a career for yourself using your own skills and interests.

HLA HLA

Hla Hla Win was born into a family of four in Yangon, Myanmar, in the early 1980s. Her parents worked for the government, which meant that they were on the bottom rung of the social ladder in their country. The family was poor, and from time to time Hla Hla was a vegetarian, not because she or her parents chose it but because the family could not afford to buy meat. In addition to their day jobs, her parents had a store, where they sold audio cassettes and rented books. Hla Hla was given the responsibility of running the store at a young age.

She became the sales manager, and her job included listening to all the cassettes and reading all the books so she could give good reviews about them. Before the internet, there was nowhere to read reviews of these books and cassettes, so her word held more weight in people's purchasing decisions, and the store was equally as popular as its sales manager. When someone came in, they were greeted by an energetic young girl who could sing the melodies of any of the cassettes and recount the events of any of the books in the shop. Hla Hla learned English from song lyrics, and reading broadened her thinking.

However, Hla Hla did not do well in school. She had a hard time focusing on anything, and it wasn't until decades later that it dawned on her that she probably had ADHD. In addition, the teachers often sent Hla Hla off to her parents' store in the middle of lessons to fetch supplies, so her studies were disjointed. Frankly, she enjoyed those errands more than her daily lessons.

After high school, Hla Hla developed an interest in becoming a travel guide, because she was fascinated by meeting tourists and hearing the stories of their lives outside Myanmar. She became the area's youngest travel guide ever, but her father did not approve of her work, so Hla Hla decided to become an English language teacher. Because school had not worked well for her, she wanted to do things differently. As a nineteen-year-old, she began teaching in her neighborhood and was given a position in a real school the next year.

However, Hla Hla wanted to learn more about educational philosophy and teaching methodologies. She wasn't satisfied with her progress and began to feel like she had to get out of the country. Hla Hla wanted to see the world she had heard about from the tourists, so she applied to ten universities in the United States, hoping for a scholarship. She was admitted to five, three of which awarded her a scholarship, one of which was a full ride with an apartment. This time Hla Hla decided to leave despite her father's opposition to the idea. She packed her bags and went to study elementary education in Iowa.

It was 2008, and the United States presidential election was in high gear. Iowa was preparing to vote, and Hla Hla saw for the first time how politics really works. She began to volunteer for Democratic candidates and met Hillary Clinton and Barack Obama during the campaign. Enthusiastic about the election, she began to work for change in her own country. After returning to Myanmar, Hla Hla became an activist, and she was heavily involved in organizing political parties for ethnic minorities.

Hla Hla was now twenty-nine, and she wanted to set up a university in Myanmar. No one believed in her idea, though, so Hla Hla decided to apply to Harvard for the fourth time. She would only return to her home country again once she had obtained sufficient qualifications that no one could doubt her abilities anymore.

A few months later, Hla Hla received two happy pieces of news: Harvard had accepted her to the Kennedy School of Education master's program with a full scholarship, and she was pregnant! However, her joy was short-lived, because she soon learned that she could not defer the beginning of her program due to the birth of her baby. She was crushed. She would be forced to forgo the long-time dream she had just achieved.

As if giving up her dreams was not enough, in the third month of her pregnancy she was diagnosed with a chronic autoimmune disease. The complications grew worse, and the doctor was forced to say words that would change Hla Hla's life forever: "You only have five years left to live." In an instant, her life was turned upside down. She could not take any medication for her condition during her pregnancy, and her relatives pressured her to have an abortion. Hla Hla began having suicidal thoughts, because her own health and the life of her child were being set against each other. However, she had to make a choice. Whether it was Harvard or her own health, the baby would come first.

Hla Hla had a girl. Like all babies, she was very demanding, but she also gave Hla Hla strength. The next year she applied again to Harvard, but this time she wrote only a very short essay, in which she said, "I don't want to have to say to my daughter one day that I gave up my dreams for her." Harvard accepted her, and the family set off with their five-month-old baby to one of the most demanding educational institutions in the world. Before long, Hla Hla graduated and came to Silicon Valley, where we met and became friends in the summer of 2016. Together we set up a company to help teachers in developing countries, staying in Silicon Valley to work together. Hla Hla wanted to do everything she could so her daughter could have a better education than she did.

It wasn't until I visited Myanmar that I really understood what a long journey she had made and how intense her entrepreneurial drive was. Whether it was teaching, politics, or founding a school, she wanted to solve every problem she saw. She dedicated years of her life and moved to the other side of the globe so she could come back and give her own daughter something better. I have so much respect for her in every aspect of life. She lives with the kind of dignity that only a truly caring person can.

I have never been so relieved as when I heard from Hla Hla that her doctor's diagnosis was recently found to be incorrect, and that she was getting well. If anyone has pushed forward against all probability, endured and overcome adversity, and shown entrepreneurship in their life, it is Hla Hla. Her surname is Win, after all. Coincidence? I think not.

360ed

We named our company 360ed, and Hla Hla took the helm with a local team in Myanmar. Soon I learned that it's very different to set up a company in Myanmar than in Finland. However, this experience has also helped me to see what all entrepreneurs around the world have in common.

Myanmar is a developing country with more than 130 ethnic groups and a political situation that has long been unstable. More than half of inhabitants work in agriculture and manufacturing, and there has been little need for education, because the same skills have been sufficient from one generation to the next. The military government has controlled the schools for decades, textbooks have not been updated for years, and censorship is strict to the point of restricting what questions are permissible to ask. Between the ages of eleven and sixteen, sixty-four percent of all children drop out of school. Reforming education in the nation will be a huge job.

However, technology has been developing in leaps and bounds. In 2012, mobile phone use was under ten percent, because a SIM card cost hundreds, sometimes even thousands of US dollars. Only five years later, in 2017, 89.9 percent of people in Myanmar were carrying a smartphone, and now it is one of the fastest-growing mobile markets in the world. This means that tens of millions of people suddenly gained access to the internet, and it almost goes without saying that a smartphone is light-years ahead of out-of-date textbooks as a learning tool.

Hla Hla, myself, and our colleague Laurent, from Canada, who joined the company later, first created 360-degree films of classrooms around the world so we could show teachers in Myanmar how contemporary pedagogy works. However, that didn't work as well as we wanted, so we began creating augmented reality mobile applications in Burmese.

We copied physics, biology, and chemistry content and converted it into teaching cards, creating convenient card decks of each subject. Then we turned the main subject elements into pictures and animations. When a student wants to learn the periodic table, for example, the application visualizes the properties of the different elements, like the atomic mass. When you show the phone the heart card from the biology deck, the student can rotate a 3-D heart to see the details better, and when they want more information, they can click a link to open Wikipedia.

The mobile application can also bring a laboratory to places where none exist physically. Students may have never been able to do chemistry experiments before, but now they can pick up petri dishes on their phone screens and do simple visual experiments to see reactions and at least get a basic sense of what the experiment is about. It's also easy to guide students to additional information on the internet, so students can get more up-to-date information than the teacher may even have.

360ed has taught me that investing in the quality of teamwork is central to success. The three of us who founded the company are all from different continents, belong to three different religions, and speak three different native languages. At the beginning we made a list of the values we were each unwilling to compromise on. This included small things like punctuality and big things like commitment. Because of the good groundwork we laid, we quickly figured out how to work productively together and achieved a lot in a short amount of time. And the more time we've spent together, the more we've discovered how similar we are.

Collaboration is at its best when everyone is teaching everyone else something unique from their own background. The more diverse the members of the team, the better they can work together if the ground rules are clear. Many times, I wondered how this same thing would have been done in Finland. But that wouldn't necessarily have been the best way for us to do it. Fortunately, we haven't always done things my way. We've discovered many universal things about learning, teaching, and children as we've each shared our own experiences. This has helped us build our ideas on issues that are common and unchanging for all of us.

WHAT CAN A DEVELOPING
COUNTRY TEACH A WELFARE STATE?

Myanmar has made a preliminary decision to digitize its old textbooks because it's more practical and cheaper than updating printed textbooks due to high mobile phone usage rates. Ten years ago, Myanmar seemed light-years away from digitalization, but the change has gone surprisingly smoothly. It's almost like the decisions have been making themselves. I once asked Hla Hla how it was possible that they had managed to make such major reforms. Education is a sensitive issue in Myanmar, after all. Where was the resistance to change? Hla Hla said that it was easy for them to try new ideas, because they had so little to lose. When you're already frequently ranked near the bottom in education and the economy compared to the rest of the world, it doesn't matter if you don't succeed completely at digitalizing education. The situation can't get radically worse than it already is. Myanmar can make bold decisions, because there is only upside. It's easier to kick off the bottom.

When I returned to Finland, that idea wouldn't leave me alone. I enjoyed not needing to squat in the bathroom or guess about when the bus might show up. There were no green lizards running around in the shower and no daily power outages. I looked around and realized how incredibly well Finland and many other welfare states are doing. We're often at the top of global comparisons, but there may also be a danger hidden in that. Are things going too well? We have such a good situation that we don't dare to try new things and risk all the good that we've managed to build. We have so much to lose. When I told Hla

Hla that an experiment like ours would cause a storm of controversy in Finland, she was astonished. "Isn't Finland one of the best?" she asked. I told her that we have so much to lose that we prefer to hold on to the past, because it works.

Or at least it used to work. Has well-being made us lazy?

The better we become, the more cautious we are. In the future, we will need the courage to experiment and implement radical ideas, even if everything is good now. The world is changing, and we can't stop the clock at today's success, because taking risks is essential for development. The fact that Finland enjoys top rankings in international measures of happiness, education, and security is something we should be proud of. But we must also remember what put us in this position. It was decisions that were made decades ago, looking into the future. Now we need the courage to make our own decisions for the next twenty years and more. Will developing countries become pioneers in some sense, because the developed world is stuck in their old systems? Will Finland become a museum to past benefits achieved?

However good or bad the starting point, you must know how to react to a changing world. Many societies have made incredible strides forward from terrible starting points. In addition to education in Myanmar, mobile payments in East Africa (an early adopter of mobile money) or e-passports in Estonia (an early innovator in biometric passports) are great examples. Many nations that, just a moment ago, looked like they had barely reached the year 2000 are now already building the 2030s.

THE GREATEST TALENT IN THE WORLD
IS SITTING IN OUR CLASSROOMS

The world is global and developing exponentially but unpredictably. Since 2010, world trade growth has been only half the average rate from 1980 to 2009. There are more trade agreements than ever, but fewer new agreements are being signed. In China, where technological development is already advanced in many places, they have a state-run economy that is among the fastest growing in the world. What do these observations tell us? It's hard to predict whether the role of the state in individuals' lives is increasing or decreasing, and whether national boundaries will be increasingly blurred in the future or whether more walls will be built. In any case, corporations are growing both their power and their responsibility.

We need a new generation of passionate entrepreneurs who operate and collaborate as themselves in a global world. Even though Finland has one of the best education systems in the world, where are our Bill Gateses, Mark Zuckerbergs, and Steve Jobses? Sitting in the desks in our classrooms, we have the best potential talent in the world. But have we succeeded in turning the world's best education system into the world's best success stories?

We need to encourage each other to take risks. This is a question of courage, of making dreams come true, and of hard work—but we already know that. In the future, entrepreneurship will become a way of life. If we don't solve the big problems, who will? Who is starting from a better position than us? Both in Myanmar and California, if things go badly, an entrepreneur can end up on the street, because there are no safety nets. And yet they still risk everything. We will have enough support for entrepreneurship when Finns start thinking about their evening plans like this: Should we have pizza or start a business?

We need to create more opportunities for children and young people to practice the skill of selling ideas and products. In the United States, kids drag a table and a chair out to a nearby intersection and sell lemonade for a dollar to passersby. Children get to try out marketing and starting a business, and they develop a sense of ownership in the sales process. In Finland we have a few fund-raisers, like scouts selling Christmas calendars, but there is plenty of room for improvement.

The experience of developing something from start to finish and then selling it is extremely rewarding. Instead of kids running bake sales outside supermarkets for their class, why not do a crowdfunding campaign online? To run a fund-raising campaign, you have to know how to tell an engaging story, justify the need for the campaign, and create a strategy for using the time available as efficiently as possible.

YOU ARE AS STRONG AS IRON! BUT DON'T RUST . . .

How do you get an idea off the ground? First you have to think about what problem you want to solve. Entrepreneurs rarely wait for inspiration. They go looking for irritants—for things that are off kilter. Identifying room for improvement is a much better starting point than waiting for inspiration. Irritation means that there is already an emotional connection to the problem and that solving it will mean something. That's your chance, but you also need passion.

Only passion will support you and help you do the amount of work that business requires.

When we create something, we also form a relationship with our creation. So, when someone criticizes your invention, it can feel like they're criticizing you. But it should never be like that. I invented the Musiclock when I was fifteen. It became something that's dear to my heart, because I put so much time into it. I was also young, so whenever someone pointed out a shortcoming in my invention or found something that needed fixing, or really criticized the idea in any way, I felt like the criticism was directed at me. I had succeeded at doing something that I was proud of, and it was a part of me.

For ages entrepreneurs have been chanting the mantra that you have to fall in love with the problem, not the solution. This helps us continue our work even when we encounter criticism. I would put the same idea a little differently, though. Search for something you love, and let it tame your ego. Don't become the creator but the midwife who brings that idea into the world.

In the future, we will need people with whom it's easy to develop new ideas. Passionate people who know how to give and receive feedback, and who are good company. In California, I learned that social skills are just as valuable as hard skills. Many of the people I met have accomplished amazing things, and I admire them greatly. But they were also really nice and personable, and they didn't make a big deal about themselves. Maybe that's why they've been able to do so much. Good things happen to good people.

We need individuals who can fall in love with the problem, endure criticism, and not shy away from failure. Men and women, young and old who dare to dream and take risks. The more uncertainty we can tolerate, the more we can enjoy this moment. Things rarely go the way we plan without any surprising twists. The strength of the entrepreneurial spirit is that it believes that every change and setback is a helpful lesson. Either we succeed or we learn.

This attitude guides us to choose the most favorable option out of the possible interpretations. Oh, we didn't get funding this time? Well, next time we'll know how to give a better pitch! Oh, the product doesn't work? Good we found out now instead of in a month! There are two kinds of things it's useless to be disappointed about: things you can't do anything about and things you can do something about. There has never been such a good time to be an entrepreneur as now.

Before, there were endeavors that only countries could attempt, like space travel. Now private companies have begun to do those things, too. Before there were activities that only private companies could accomplish, like setting up online stores, but now anyone can do that in a few minutes from their couch. Opportunity has moved closer to the individual, and new technologies offer a tremendous number of ways to influence public issues. If you can do something about whatever it is, don't worry—get to work!

Remember, even if a task looked impossible yesterday and today someone criticizes your idea, tomorrow it might change the world. It doesn't have to be easy; it just has to be possible. Believe in yourself and remember that almost nothing can break iron but its own rust.

FUTURE WORK

- Don't waste a good crisis! It's giving you an excellent opportunity to learn something.

- Think of yourself as an entrepreneur. Entrepreneurship is an attitude.

- Believe in your dreams and create your own path.

- If something could be done better, don't be a bystander. Do it!

- Have the courage to take responsibility for yourself and learn to sell your ideas.

- Be the one everyone wants to work with.

9 PERSEVERANCE AND PATIENCE

A world that loves quick fixes and easy wins needs perseverance, because only commitment brings success.

If you want to accomplish something important in your life, you should learn to be persistent and patient. The most important things require systematic planning, effort, perseverance, and stick-to-itiveness. Friendship, love, trust, and success do not come overnight.

Despite this, we live in a time of instant payday loans. We've forgotten what patience is because our environment, with all its services and products, has been designed to give us solutions immediately and effortlessly. Technology has made our lives easier, but fast and easy solutions can't become the norm. If you want to get the cake out of the oven faster, don't turn the temperature up or you'll burn it. You have to set the heat low and wait patiently.

Things you can get fast are not as lasting as the ones you have to work for. When we're just cramming for tomorrow's test, we forget everything once it's done, but try to forget something you've spent weeks patiently studying. That you get to keep. Learning some things takes months, years, or even half a lifetime, but those are the things we learn properly. The challenge is that because of the spread of instant gratification from the entertainment industry into everyday tasks, we can't stand such slow development. We prefer to maximize and optimize everything.

I believe that boredom is important sometimes, perhaps even essential. And yet we continue to try to make everything fun, and our tolerance for a moment of boredom is almost nonexistent. Relaxation, enjoyment, and entertainment are important, but not all the time. Has an abundant life deprived us of patience? Stories about our parents' and grandparents' childhoods make it sound like they didn't give up easily, even if some things required a lot of effort. Now when grocery bags show up at the front door at the press of a button, laundry service can be ordered using an app, and we can chat with friends without even getting out of bed, we get bored the instant the internet slows down or any service is temporarily unavailable.

We probably don't forget anything faster than those things we should be grateful for. Adversity is a good reminder. As I was writing this book, I broke three bones in my foot, and walking with crutches forced me to slow down my life. But the boredom I experienced taught me patience. I don't intend to rush so much anymore once I get my foot back.

Our time is our most important resource. We have to actively remember to concentrate on the aspects of life that are worth our attention. We need to define as valuable those things for which we're ready to endure a little more for a little longer. You know that one friend who isn't on social media? Take a little extra effort to tell him how you're doing and invite him to your party, too. Even if things aren't easy or don't go according to plan, that doesn't mean you shouldn't do them.

We can't give up at the first sign of a problem or change our minds whenever something more attractive comes along. Confidence in long-term results is central to our success, and we need to be able to say yes to the right things and no to others. Without commitment, there is no depth. Persistence brings meaning, and patience is a virtue. Luckily, these are skills that can be learned. There's nothing more rewarding than long-term work that bears fruit. I promise that your quality of life will improve if you exercise patience.

WHERE DOES PERSISTENCE COME FROM?

The part of my life that has taught me the most persistence is cello lessons. When I was practicing my body and finger positions, I did hundreds of repetitions and practiced every day for years. That work requires tenacity. I hit more than one wall during my early musical career, and my parents got an earful plenty of times about how I didn't feel like practicing. But now, as an adult, the ability to play the cello is one of my greatest joys. Anyone who admires the beautiful sounds and melodies of my cello is actually admiring the fifteen years of dedicated practice that got me here. I never could have imagined how pleased I would be as an adult that sometimes I gritted my teeth and pushed through.

But the tenacity didn't come out of nowhere. Motivation is the elixir of persistence and patience. Whenever we feel like stopping and giving up, we've usually lost touch with what we originally set out to do. The decision to keep going or to stop depends on whether the long-term reward is important enough. As a child, I had no goals related to playing the cello, and it's entirely understandable that practicing the correct positions of my finger joints sometimes felt mind-numbing. Even if someone had told me that someday I would be able to play for my friends in the park on summer nights, I still probably would have chosen my Pokémon. But my parents and teacher were able to use small prizes to get me through the worst phase. Children don't think very far into the future, but adults can—if they've really grown up. Another skill related to persistence and patience is the ability to remember the reasons we tackle certain goals.

What we spend our time on depends on our choices, and our choices depend on our values. It's easy to make choices when we know our values, but if we don't know what our values are, we're lost. When I was deciding which high school to go to, I had to make up my mind whether I would focus on sports or music. This choice wasn't just difficult, it was downright traumatic. However, it forced me to consider my values and what was important to me. I was at the height of my sports career, but I knew that music would give me more in the long run. Once I was clear about my values, it was easy for me to say yes to music. Today when I find myself in a similar situation, where I have to make a difficult choice, I use the same thinking. If I don't immediately know what to do, there's usually a deeper conflict. I think for a moment, and then the choice is easy. It's always a value judgment.

So, persistence requires reflection so you can find your core values and the reasons for your actions. No one can be persistent without goals and dreams. They need to be significant, because if a dream is big enough, we'll give it everything we have. Working to achieve goals that are bigger than yourself is better than focusing on your own interests. When the chips are down, a goal like becoming famous won't help you nearly as much as a goal like helping others and increasing understanding. It is only once we've worked toward goals that are bigger than our own egos that we are rewarded with the sense of meaning that helps us to be persistent. In the 1960s, there was a NASA janitor who said that what motivated him in his work was that they were sending a man to the moon. Actually, more than four hundred thousand people were working toward that same goal, and they all felt like they were part of something greater than themselves.

A future in which we don't commit to big goals is too myopic for real growth. Persistence begins when we know what we're working for and periodically remind ourselves. Everything is hard in the beginning. It took me two years before playing the cello was interesting enough that I took responsibility for it myself. Now I'm thankful to my persistent parents, who didn't give up on me. Their great hope was that one day I would see that all that work was worth the effort.

HIGH JUMPERS WILL SUCCEED IN THE FUTURE

What makes people equal is that we all have twenty-four hours in the day. In everything else, we're in different situations. Nationality, family, gender, hobbies, opportunities, and our stations in life put us on different starting lines in this lifelong marathon. However, we still have those twenty-four hours in common. We can't change what kind of send-off we got in life, but we are ultimately responsible for how we spend the time allotted to us. In ten years, will you be satisfied with the things you did this week? You can't succeed at ten years until you succeed at twenty-four hours, because the wise use of time and persistent work lead to success.

However, too often success in life is associated with recognition. It isn't until we see someone standing on the winner's podium that we call them successful. But success is ultimately a remarkably simple thing. It comes from just barely clearing the bar. Even great accomplishments are the result of repeating small habits and routines. When you repeat a few good actions every day, the results start to show. The difference between success and failure comes from small things that accumulate over days, weeks, months, and years. According to one estimate, each adult makes about seventy choices a day. Either you're earning interest or piling up debt that you'll see ten years later in your account. In order to clear that bar each day, you need persistence.

Success is the wisdom to make small decisions over the long term, and patience is the tolerance for the work that must be done to achieve a goal. Every morning when I wake up, I try to think about one, and only one, important thing that I want to get done that day. If I get it done, then I can say the day was good. Many people ponder the meaning of life, but they don't understand that whatever that is, it should also be important to them today. How we spend our days is ultimately how we spend our lives. A good life is made up of a series of good days. Can you say what makes a day good?

I don't always succeed at even doing that one thing, but in the end the question isn't just whether I achieved my goal on that particular day or not. When I ask myself what the most important task is to get done, it forces me to think and focus my intentions. I have to face who I am and what I want. Usually just saying the question out loud teaches me something. Repeated every day, the lesson eventually hits home.

Forming new habits feels difficult at first, but if you're tenacious, one day you'll wake up and realize your new habits have become part of everyday life. There is no middle ground. Success is cultivated one day at a time—those twenty-four hours that we all have in common. Be persistent like a high jumper and always raise the bar a little at a time, so you're just barely passing over it!

WHAT SHOULD I ASPIRE TO? NOT HAPPINESS!

One of the differences between happiness and meaning is that one of them is easy to get and the other is hard. If you want to be happy for a while, you can do it by buying a new phone, going on a beach vacation, or singing along with the crowd at a music festival. There are an endless number of different ways to be happy. However, if your new phone breaks, the weather is terrible on your vacation, or your favorite singer cancels their performance, your happiness just as quickly fades.

Meaning, on the other hand, is difficult because it requires patience and effort. There are not an endless number of ways to make life meaningful, and finding them requires reflection. However, meaning in life cannot be taken away from you, even if your beach vacation is canceled.

We shouldn't strive for happiness; we should strive for meaning. There's no point getting too wrapped up in anything that can be taken away from you. It isn't a question of what you want to enjoy, it's about what problems you want to endure. And often happiness is about us, while meaning can only be gained through other people. Instead of striving for happiness and admiration, we should seek solutions and patience. Wittgenstein said that we should not seek people's respect but rather their love. Respect is related to what you are and loving to what you do. In other words, respect might bring happiness, but loving will bring meaning. For example, if you're a leader, many people may respect you, but what would you have to do as a leader for people to love you?

The difference between happiness and meaning is persistence and patience. Quick solutions and the pursuit of abundance don't give us meaning, even though we've been sold the idea that the ecstasy of the moment is the same thing as meaning. In the pursuit of abundance, we want more and more of what we don't even really need. It's no longer enough just to watch a movie. Now we have to have candy and popcorn, just the right friends, dinner beforehand, drinks afterward, and of course social media updates so everyone else can comment on what a nice evening we had. Only too much is enough.

Our attitude toward disappointment can also show us whether or not we're striving for meaning or happiness. Failure is always unfortunate, but meaningful things are more resistant to adversity. Often one single event can put us in a bad mood, and if we aren't careful, it can ruin the happiness of our whole day. But when something is meaningful, we continue despite failures, and one bad day isn't going to make us quit. We all have bad days, but there is often something good to be found even in a bad day, if we look closely enough. In truth, there are no bad days, only bad moments. One failure does not ruin the whole thing if you're doing something that is meaningful to you.

When we're striving for the right goals, we can stick with it through the hard times, too. Patience means consciously putting off satisfying our needs. The farther off we succeed at shifting the reward, the better it feels. Unfortunately, digital services are now able to build in very subtle reward mechanisms that attempt to prey on our time. How often do you grab your phone for no particular reason?

In the future, we'll need to be able to focus patiently on one thing at a time, even if it feels boring. Not everything can or should be made into an addictive game or social media app. Happiness is not a trophy case. Sometimes we get bored or our nerves are frazzled, but persistence pays. That's the difference between happiness and meaning. We don't need to fear failure. What we need to fear is collecting prizes for success at something that ultimately has no meaning.

HISTORY REMEMBERS PERSISTENT PEOPLE

History remembers persistent people. When you think of giants of history like Nelson Mandela, Martin Luther King Jr., Mother Teresa, or Gandhi, do you think of a rash person who jumped only the lowest hurdle? No, of course not. These were all people who did more than was asked of them. They started with small things, which, repeated day by day, brought them and others great good.

These small things are simple, everyday habits. They may include waking up earlier, studying harder, exercising more regularly, or having the courage to buck expectations. Persistence is about self-leadership. The earlier we learn to lead ourselves, the greater the thanks we will end up giving to our past selves. If your heart wants to learn some new skill, go to the library and study. If your heart wants to become a singer, go take singing lessons and practice. Take yourself where you want to go. Move your butt to where your heart is.

As a people, we Finns have had the grit to do the long-term work necessary to put us at the top of international comparisons, whether we're talking about education, security, or happiness. We can thank past generations, because their choices, decisions, and above all their efforts have given us the prosperity we now enjoy. It's good to remember that just over one hundred years ago, the average life expectancy for a person living in Finland was only forty-six, GDP was at the same level as in Tanzania today, and only five percent of the population studied beyond elementary school. Finland was still receiving development aid until the mid-1960s.

Now it's our job to continue that tenacious work for the common good as we face unprecedented global and technological upheavals, which challenge our education system, our security, and our happiness. Now we must make the same kinds of wise decisions so the next generation can celebrate in 2050 more than 130 years of Finnish history, not just the first one hundred years. So that they can say of us, *they sure were brave and wise back then in the 2020s as they reacted to the challenges of a changing world.*

The future will require quick action and momentum, but that does not preclude determination and commitment. When something is wrong, we often look for the quickest relief instead of being ready to make the long-term repairs that will really fix the issue. In a world where everything is available instantly, we have become impatient. The internet has made us demand everything in a click or two. Now we need to develop persistence and patience, and above all decide what values we're working for. We must set an example for each other that persistence is worthwhile. Let's start with small goals but grow them persistently over time. Let's do the long-term work needed to leave a better world for those who come after us.

FUTURE WORK

- Think about the single most important thing you need to do today.

- Do a few small things well, but do them every day.

- Don't tire yourself out for a small goal. Dare to dream big.

- Remind yourself of why you do what you do. Keep the goal in mind.

- If something goes wrong, don't let one moment ruin your whole day.

- Don't let the pursuit of happiness fool you. Do something that matters.

10 | WELL-BEING AND SELF-KNOWLEDGE

If your mind and body are unhealthy, you can't develop future skills. You have to take care of yourself.

I magine that you're sitting in a chair, leaning back so the chair is balanced on two legs. If you lean just a little, you remain in control of the situation and can return to a normal position. However, there is a critical point as you lean back after which gravity will pull the chair down and you will fall. Past that point, you can't regain your balance no matter how hard you try. As you fall, the speed of the chair increases until you impact the floor.

Life is the same. We lean and we push ourselves toward a critical point, sometimes harder, sometimes more gently. However, sometimes we lean too far, pass the critical point, and get sick, mentally or physically. Then we need others' help to get back up.

Is it possible that digitalization is pushing us to lean ever farther back in the chair, past a critical point toward a collapse of our well-being? There are already warning signs. Our ability to concentrate has diminished, addictions are more common, and mental illnesses are on the rise. The Institute for Health Metrics Evaluation (IHME) estimates that around thirteen percent of people globally are already suffering from mental health problems, and the World Health Organization predicts that by 2030 these ailments will be one of the major causes of the worldwide disease burden. In addition, obesity has already nearly tripled since 1975. What's going on?

Technological change has undoubtedly played a part in this development, because it has radically altered our behavior. Consider all the things that can happen in the span of a single person's life now—and how that changes our actions. Just over a decade ago, we didn't need social media or streaming services, but now they feel like irreplaceable everyday entertainment without which few people would know how to live or even want to live. Technology has helped us in many ways, but it has not necessarily made life more meaningful. Digitalization will only continue to accelerate, and that may lead to an overwhelming sense of malaise. The predictions are already concerning.

Well-being and self-awareness will be extremely important skills in the future because they help us navigate a changing world of unpredictable environments. We need self-awareness so we can recognize the fears and insecurities that change awakens in us. We need an understanding of what well-being really is and tools for tolerating uncertainty. Uncertainty should not be an obstacle to happiness. Actually, the more uncertainty you tolerate now, the better your chances are of being satisfied with how things turn out.

It may be that we have only seen the tip of the iceberg of what the transition to a digital and global world will cause for us. Old thought patterns and habits may no longer apply in the future, so we need to relearn the fundamentals of well-being. New expectations, pressures, needs, and demands are being placed on us. Believing in our own abilities and that we can succeed in a changing world is critical. Instead of becoming victims of change, we can see change as an opportunity to improve our well-being and to jump into something new.

A LEAP INTO THE UNKNOWN

They say that stupidity multiplies in a group, but it depends on the point of view. I think enthusiasm intensifies in a group. The following is a story about enduring uncertainty and believing in one's own abilities.

One day while I was in California, I saw an advertisement for a group discount for parachuting. I showed it to my friends, and we decided to take the leap. In retrospect, skydiving may not be the best service to haggle about the price of, just for the sake of safety. But as I said, enthusiasm intensifies in a group—or stupidity. Skydiving is common in California, and a lot of people have done it at some point in their lives. And besides, it's safer than driving a car, because many more people die in traffic. By that logic, we had no reason to worry.

A couple of days before blastoff, we heard that two young men had died in Southern California as a result of a skydiving accident. Their chutes had not opened properly, and the jumpers landed in an apple orchard. There were dramatic images of tattered parachutes in the news articles. Our first reaction was fear. Could I have been that young man? Is jumping safe when it's cheap? One person in our group immediately decided to stay home, at his wife's request, and the rest of us had to think hard about what to do. The enthusiastic mood had suddenly taken a whole new turn, but we reasoned that two accidents couldn't happen so close together. That would be an astonishing coincidence if it did. Humor helped us cope with the extra tension brought on by the accident. We thought that in case we died, we needed to come up with a motto that would then be shared around the world with the news and make us ambassadors for peace: "Drop people, not bombs!" In retrospect, it was pretty morbid.

At the airport, I had to sign a paper denying my next of kin any legal recourse or compensation in case of an accident. Suddenly the threat of failure crept back into my mind, and I forgot all my logic about safety and probabilities. The jump was done in tandem, and I was paired up with a jumper who never took his sunglasses off. It would have inspired more confidence to see the eyes of the person who would take responsibility for my life in fifteen minutes, but I just had to trust blindly. However, on the waiting room wall there were pictures of thousands of past jumps.

Our tiny rattletrap plane climbed into the sky, and when we reached the right altitude, the door opened. I moved to the edge and sat, looking down between my legs. My stomach lurched. On the horizon I could see the Pacific Ocean and the bright California sun. Below were thousands of meters of nothing. I looked at my friends one last time, now blind with excitement, counted to three with my partner, and tumbled over the edge into the sky. I started screaming at the top of my lungs. Screaming is actually recommended, so breathing is easier while you're in free fall. Although I doubt anyone in that situation is doing it out of a compulsion to follow the instructions.

The jump was a wonderful experience. In the air you feel an indescribable, ephemeral sense of peace. You just fall, speeding and spinning downward. Even though the wind is rushing at you like you're standing on top of a car on a freeway, it is amazingly quiet.

This experience gave me the best lesson of my life about how to maintain calm in a situation that is out of the ordinary and maybe even a bit extreme. It forced me to focus on the feelings moving through my mind and body, which were heightened by the accident that had happened just before our jump. When the world changes, we have to be able to maintain our peace of mind and control our fears. Uncertainty requires courage.

The jump taught me what the philosopher Seneca observed around two thousand years ago: "We suffer more often in imagination than in reality." Statistics and probabilities don't help, because our fears are constructions of our minds, and often irrational ones at that. I had no reason to be afraid until I started running worst-case scenarios. Without imagination, we could never do anything, but sometimes it makes life harder. People who have active, vibrant imaginations see more shadows and fears than they need to. That's why people with rich imaginations need even more courage to take action. Fear is often just a misuse of imagination.

THE FUTURE IS A CONTROL FREAK'S WORST NIGHTMARE

Skydiving taught me to momentarily let go of control and trust in the expertise of another person. That's a difficult skill to master, but it would help us a lot in life. We feel empowered when we can influence the circumstances around us through our own actions. The fact that we can make conscious efforts to effect positive change in our lives may be the most encouraging thing I know. The cornerstone of mental health is a sense of control, the confidence that you can make your own life better. You can. Without hope for the better, we would not be able to look into the future.

Your future will look inspiring or scary depending on whether you believe in your ability to handle a changing world. It's hard to find joy when you can't influence events in your own life. The opposite of a sense of control is the feeling that everything could disappear at any moment. Unexpected events undercut the sense of control. Certainty helps us be happy, and uncertainty takes it away from us.

This idea about control is changing now, though. In an uncertain future, we will need to be able to tolerate the fact that we cannot control everything. Our happiness can no longer be based on predictability.

Before there were certain rules of the game, and you could build your whole life on them. Get this education, and you get that job. Get these skills, and you'll get paid that much. We could calculate, make decisions, and trust how they would play out. In the future, rules like this will no longer hold throughout anyone's entire life. There is no template that will serve with the same certainty as before. Parents have always wanted a secure profession for their children, but there are no secure professions anymore.

Work is changing, industries are being revolutionized, education is in upheaval, and technology is creating new jobs as it destroys the old. No matter what degree you earn today, there is no guarantee that it will get you a job for the next thirty years. In thirty years, if a current profession still exists, the job description may have changed so radically that an old degree won't guarantee the required skills. People have always needed to adapt to change, but now we must tolerate more of it than previous generations. The rules of the game might cover a few decades at most.

Maybe instead of change, we should talk about development, so the future doesn't feel so negative. It's great that the world is developing more during our lifetimes than ever before! That's why this is the best time in human history to be alive. We get to witness new scientific breakthroughs, see the emergence of new industries, and be lifelong learners. The other side of the coin just happens to be that even though you do everything right, get straight As, and land a prestigious job, we can no longer promise you a guaranteed future. The way the world is changing—excuse me—developing forces us to give up control. The question is now what attitude you take to your future.

The earlier we learn to be happy surrounded by surprises, unpredictable changes, and new currents, the better our future will be. In the future, the basis for our well-being will be tolerance for uncertainty and faith in our own abilities. An evolving person is happy person. Change shouldn't rob us of meaning, it should enable it.

COMPARISON IS A BAD HOBBY

The psychologist Leon Festinger observed that we compare ourselves to others to eliminate uncertainty. Because we find change fundamentally suspicious, we compare our own situation with others. This gives us a point of reference and makes choices feel safer. Should I accept that job or not?

Should I get into a relationship with this person? Is that the best possible vacation spot? In order to answer questions like this, we consider what others would do in the same situation. If other people see a job, a relationship, or a vacation destination as desirable, then I should choose it. This helps us prop up our self-esteem a bit, eliminate uncertainty, and make decisions slightly more easily. It's typical of human nature to compare ourselves to others. Social media and the entertainment industry depend on this. Facebook was originally built to allow college students to compare each other's pictures and profiles. Whether it's a face, a comment, or a status, we want to feel a little better than someone else. In a twisted way, comparison can make us feel more unique, but it also prevents us from enjoying what we have.

I hate comparisons. It feels like they are the root of all evil, because even if everything is fine for us, comparing ourselves to others makes us feel like it isn't enough. In a world where we're in contact with ever-increasing numbers of people, someone always has more. But I believe that we will become happier by wanting less. How long will it take to learn to enjoy what we have? The answer to the question of whether the glass is half-full or half-empty is that there's water in the glass, and you can drink it.

I've received my best lessons about comparison when I've spent time with people I really look up to. When I arrived for a summer seminar at Singularity University in Silicon Valley, I knew in advance what amazing people would be in my group. During the first couple of days, I got to experience some serious impostor syndrome. I felt so strongly that I didn't belong there. The people around me were such amazing geniuses with such huge accomplishments and fantastic stories that I felt like someone had made a huge mistake in choosing me. But when the organizers asked us all how many of us felt like that, I was surprised when almost every hand shot up. Even the ones I would have rated highest out of all of us said that they were starting to doubt their own abilities.

Comparison and judging our abilities never ends. No matter what unbelievable things we've done in our lives, we can never get away from impostor syndrome. A similar situation happened at the Nobel Festival. Over the course of the week, we participated in a range of different activities, each more incredible than the last. Having dinner with the Nobel laureates and chatting with the discoverer of the Higgs boson, Peter Higgs, himself, was literally unbeatable. I was so happy to get to have experiences like that, because they taught me to compare less. You can't construct a life out of highs like that. Not everything can be a Nobel dinner. We have to learn to enjoy the basics of normal, everyday life.

If we're always looking for a new, higher summit, we'll get hooked on the wrong things. Many of us spend our whole lives striving for something better and never learn to take joy in what's already around us. Many celebrities have said that they think pursuing celebrity is absurd. You hope you'll get it until you do and then learn how pointless it is. A lot of actors have admitted that winning an Oscar sent them into depression. Even the greatest award won't fill that hole. It will only make it more visible.

Kevin Carter was a photographer who received a Pulitzer Prize for his work but died by suicide only a few months later. If only we could realize as early as possible that achievements and accolades will not bring us happiness by themselves. The most important thing is the work you've done to earn them. The winner of the comparison competition will get the prize but win nothing. If a snail wins a snail race, it's still a snail. Don't be a snail!

SOCIAL MEDIA IS FAST FOOD

Comparison has become the new plague of our time, eating away at our psychological well-being. The internet has given us a new space in which to judge, belittle, and disparage but also to admire, adore, and marvel at other people. Our comparisons are no longer limited to the residents of our own villages—we have the whole world now. We can compare strangers to each other or to ourselves.

Instead of setting ourselves up against classmates, now our standards are set by Instagram celebrities whose lives (or at least the highlights) we follow through our screens. Social media would probably break down entirely if we stopped comparing ourselves this way. Social media apps are designed to make us spend as much time on their services as possible. We want to see what's happening in other people's lives, and we unconsciously compare our own lives to what we observe.

Before, teenagers were mostly raised by their parents and the surrounding community, which consisted of schoolmates, neighbors, and relatives. Now teens are being taught by other teens on attention-oriented commercial platforms, i.e., social media, which has become a sort of secret parent. Instead of a safe, familiar circle of acquaintances, now we're dealing with strangers on the app du jour.

This phenomenon is new, and we have no long-term longitudinal studies about the effects of social media. How-

ever, we can assume that this will not be a fleeting phenomenon: new trends and services will break through in the
years to come, and we will start using them. It may be that
in two years you'll be hooked on a service that hasn't been
developed yet. Do you remember the time before Facebook?
Maybe you'll look back on today with the same nostalgia in
a few years. Was life "better" before Facebook? Will it also
be "better" now than in a few years?

Perhaps in the future part of well-being will be the limiting of social media services, because the use of social media
does not seem to make us happier. The World Health Organization has estimated that half of mental illnesses are now
starting in people under the age of fourteen. That is a hor-
rifying number. We must identify what we really require in
order to connect to other people in the digital age. We may
be getting what we want from these services, but not what
we need. Fast food fills our bellies temporarily, but there are
better alternatives to starvation.

I'm not saying that we have to stop using social media,
but I am encouraging us to compare ourselves less to other
people. I'm not saying that screen time needs to be limited, but I am recommending that we consider whether
our digital devices are taking more than they're giving us.
It's hard to see this culture of comparison fading any time
soon. Quite the opposite. It is spreading into every aspect
of our lives. We're moving toward a world in which everything that can be measured will be measured and compared. The expectations, demands, and pressures arising
from these comparisons will increase. How effective are
you at work? How healthy are you? How much do you
sleep? How much do you exercise? And on and on. It will

be left to us to decide whether this information is making us happier or not.

GET A HOUSEPLANT NOW!

If you don't have houseplants in your immediate vicinity, get one right away. Caring for a plant can teach you many things. Watch how it stands up straight and tall. Confidently reaching ever higher, it feels no fear. It may even be a little proud of its stem, as long as it remembers its roots. It doesn't bother comparing itself to other plants. It remembers where it came from and the smell of dirt. It focuses on the essentials and remembers the basics: it's important to drink water regularly, whether the jug is half-empty or half-full.

A houseplant focuses on the fundamentals and doesn't give in to the need for instant gratification. It thinks big, remembers its growth potential, and is happy with how much it has progressed thus far. It enjoys fresh air and gets plenty of sun. It remembers that the weather isn't always good and the winter can freeze anyone, no matter how strong. Digitization can make everyday life distressing, but a houseplant can let go of dead leaves, aka, drop unnecessary social media services. A houseplant knows how to look around and enjoy the scenery. Just be still, stop, listen to the silence, and do nothing.

Get a houseplant, and it will remind you of these things every day. When we reflect, we have the opportunity to learn more about what's good for us and what's not. Moving forward in life comes from emotional growth, and emotional growth does not take place without self-knowledge. If well-being was a car, self-knowledge would be the fuel.

We should never be in such a hurry that we don't have time to refuel.

Busyness is self-inflicted. Remember to be merciful to yourself. If you want to do more in your life, slow down a little.

FUTURE WORK

- Stop. You must be able to interpret your emotional state before you can improve it.

- Take your brain out for a walk. Like a dog, every day. Take your mind for a jog.

- Give up control, enjoy uncertainty, and live in the moment.

- Think about whether your fears are just tricks of your imagination. Be brave!

- Don't compare. Other people's lives look better online than they really are.

- Keep the basics in order, even when you're in a rush. Don't shortchange your well-being.

11 COMPASSION AND HONESTY

The future may be better than this moment only if we know how to step into others' shoes.

Who wouldn't want every generation to be more compassionate and honest than the previous one? These qualities are unanimously considered good and desirable. The more technological our society becomes, the more humane it will also become—or at least it should. As a counterbalance to automation and algorithms, we need the ability to understand what is valuable in humanity, and because of that, compassion and honesty will become increasingly important. Technology has helped us address challenges related to food, health, and other basic needs, which has reduced suffering in the world. But on the other hand, technology, like social media, has also been used to fuel hatred. Without compassion and honesty, even good tools can turn bad.

As the world unites, the people we need to get along with will no longer be restricted to our neighborhood, village, or country. In a globalized world, we have to be able to get along with people who represent very different cultures, beliefs, and philosophies. In this environment, we will need the ability to show compassion for others, but at the same time the ability to be honest with ourselves about who we are. Honesty leads to compassion, and compassion leads to honesty.

We all live in our own unique reality. We perceive different things around us and think about ideas and events in our own ways. It's impossible to create a connection with someone if we don't strive to understand their reality and perspective. Only when we actively try to see another person's reality can we step into it and show that we're trying to connect. Only when we learn to treat everyone with equality and fairness can we become more tolerant. I firmly believe that the capacity for compassion will be the strongest asset for success in the future. Develop compassion and everything else will follow.

Honesty will also be a strong currency in the future. It saves time and resources and can prevent conflict. Only an honest person can create a behavioral change in someone else. What do you think of telemarketers? Even if they ask how you're doing, you know what their intentions are, and you don't like talking to them. Young people are especially sensitive to recognizing when you're trying to sell them something. When we discover someone trying to force a product or idea on us, it only pushes us away. But when a salesperson is honest about their intentions, their chances improve.

The importance of honesty is growing, because we are increasingly able to differentiate between genuine and false interactions. We know how to recognize pretense and acting, so influencing other people using the old methods doesn't work anymore. If you want to sell something, tell people that you're about to start an advertisement. If you want to get other people to do something, be honest about your intentions. In a world optimized by algorithms, we will develop an ever-greater need for genuineness and authenticity. For me, honesty is genuine and authentic. We're increasingly good at maintaining a certain image of ourselves for others, but I believe that the need for authenticity will only be accentuated in the coming decades.

YOU'RE THE SUM OF THE PEOPLE YOU HAVE MET DURING YOUR LIFE

As social individuals, we humans are essentially the sum of all the people we have met during our lives. Let's assume that we have meaningful interactions with five people each day for eighty years. During one lifetime, this would mean being in dialogue 146,000 times. Let's assume that every situation, every individual, and every interaction leaves a small imprint on us. We always meet the next person with the unique experience base we have at that moment.

Let's assume that someday machines are able to interpret human word choices and tones of voice. The machine would understand which word is appropriate to use in each situation and would be able to interpret the different meanings of a word based on what tone it was spoken in. Word X said in way Y means that the speaker's real feeling about the issue is Z. If this was possible, the machine (for example, Siri or Alexa) would have contact with humans around the world millions of times each day. Where a person is the sum of 146,000 encounters, the machine would have a million conversations during a single day. In one day, the machine could become a better interpreter, therapist, and comforter than any of us as a result of its vastly more rapid learning ability. If I told the machine that I had a crappy day today, it would know how to interpret from my intonation whether I'm more sad or angry, as well as defining what I really mean by the word *crappy*. For example, it might know with 92.7 percent certainty what I'm feeling, only because it had already had thousands of similar experiences. This being the case, it would know how best to respond, as well as what will cheer me up.

What could this mean in practice? For example, no head of state can chat with every citizen they represent, but a machine could quickly create an analysis of what the people are really thinking. So why couldn't the machine be the ruler or the leader? Would a voice and a face on a screen be enough for us? It could listen to people's complaints every day and give suggestions, ask opinions, and analyze emotional states. People would feel like the AI leader understood them, because it would say the right things at the right time.

However, compassion is not just about saying the right things at the right time. At its core, compassion is about what one person can fundamentally give to another person. Leaders often inspire through their own conduct, which is why a virtual leader would be unlikely to enjoy much support. An AI leader might make more right decisions than a person, but a real leader shows their vulnerability and admits their mistakes, which increases our confidence in them.

By looking in each other's eyes, we can say more than words can capture. Our body language can communicate things that aren't conveyed by the emphasis of our words. It isn't enough to remember a few phrases of condolence that we might say to someone who has lost a family member. We must learn to be genuinely present, person to person. The interpretation has to be more subtle. The compassion and honesty must be genuine.

In certain situations, a machine can act as a listener when we need one. Research has shown that it may be easier to talk to a machine than a human about difficult issues. In one study, patients described their symptoms and side effects from medications more honestly to a machine than to a person. People told the machine the facts about their ailments, but they downplayed them to the doctors. Soldiers returning from war also preferred to tell their experiences to a machine than to another person. In another study about soldiers, researchers found that the threshold for seeking help for mental health–related problems was lower when the other party was a machine rather than a human.

Asking for help is often seen as a sign of weakness, and the presence of the machine removed this feeling for the soldiers. The anonymity afforded by the machine also eased fears that asking for help would negatively impact their future in the military. It was as if the stories were disappearing into the void with no one listening or judging. There was just this machine, which had been programmed to show compassion.

There are things that need to be said out loud, but that we can't bear to hear the answers to. Do you want machines to be compassionate? If not, then at least you won't be disappointed with unrealistic expectations. Either way, machines have already opened a pathway for getting people to be more honest. Is it that we could create a safe and compassionate enough space to talk about difficult things, but we don't always succeed? Or is a machine a superior listener because it is more compassionate than a person?

CAN MACHINES GIVE US COMFORT?

This question is much more complex than you might assume at first glance. One of the most interesting things about the development of robotics is that the further the industry pushes, the more it reveals about us as humans. We're developing robots to understand ourselves better. A machine has no consciousness or emotions, but it can act the same way an empathetic person would act. Is that enough for us?

Throughout history, we have replaced people with machines. In the time before traffic lights, it might have seemed questionable to give such a big responsibility as a congested intersection to a machine. How could we let a machine decide who gets to drive when? And what if someone gets killed? The more subtle machines become, the more often they perform our jobs. We're already at the mercy of machines in many areas, and we rely on them much more than we often realize. But do we feel that tasks like providing consolation should only belong to people? We couldn't let a machine do *that*!

We aren't all particularly good listeners, and we aren't always able to give comfort or to be present as well as we could. Could a machine be a better version of us? Could we get used to machine comfort just like we got used to traffic lights? Both take advantage of machine learning. When we have a bad day, a machine can be taught to say the right things at the right time. But will that be enough for us?

At least so far, technology has only increased the need for genuine human interaction, and I believe that will continue to be the case. On the other hand, technology has also given us new opportunities to develop our empathy skills.

Imagine putting virtual reality glasses on and jumping into the middle of a battlefield. What do you see? How does it feel? Imagine opening your eyes in a hospital where nurses dressed in protective clothing are treating patients with a deadly virus. You blink your eyes and suddenly you're in a kindergarten class witnessing children's delight as they succeed in building structures out of dry spaghetti with a marshmallow on top.

It's ironic that technological devices both create a need for compassion and seek to fill it. However, experiencing the above situations even virtually can leave deep impressions on the thinking of both young and old. Virtual reality can be a sort of compassion vending machine that gives us the opportunity to understand another person's reality better. When used properly, technology can do tremendous good. It can create an entirely new impetus to the development of emotional intelligence.

A machine can give comfort, at least to a certain point, but it can also teach us how to give comfort, at least to a certain point. The subtle nuances, which are the most important things, will still be left to us to interpret, though. And those are the details in which real connection hides.

CAN THERE BE TOO MUCH COMPASSION?

Concepts that are seen exclusively as positive or negative deserve critical scrutiny simply because we all agree on them. In colloquial speech, pity, sympathy, empathy, compassion, and altruism tend to be confused, but we see them all as important. Especially when it comes to empathy, we tend to think that the more, the better. And while it is one of the most important future skills, there are also problems associated with it. Empathy can be myopic, biased, and self-ish. Professor of psychology Paul Bloom from Yale University has explored the nuances of empathy and claims that it can actually be dangerous. How, you ask?

Empathy can be used as a conscious tool of power, because it is based on imagination. We are more often influenced by emotions than statistics. Feelings beat facts, because humans are an emotional apparatus that can also think, not the other way around. Many decisions have been based on the story of a single individual or some other anecdotal piece of information. For example, if we hear about a teacher who is trying a new pedagogical method but has a student who can barely even read, we feel frustrated on behalf of the student. If the media catches hold of this single case, huge numbers of people will instantly criticize the new teaching method. But in doing so, we would be forgetting that according to the 2015 PISA survey, eleven percent of Finnish elementary school leavers could not read at the grade level required for the next level of school. This teacher's aim was to improve this status quo, and after the experiment there was only one student in the class who didn't reach the goal. And yet the story made us feel resistant to the experiment, even though the results backed it up.

Empathy is also shortsighted. Having an illiterate student in your own child's school feels worse than the same thing on the other side of the country. The immediate negative, that being the drop in the student's grade this year, makes us criticize the teaching method, and we don't see the positive effects that might be waiting at the end of middle school. We pay more attention to what's close to us and evaluate based on short-term results, because we are guided by emotion. Empathy can turn us into irrational people and bad decision makers.

The other challenge for empathy is that we don't experience it equally. We feel more empathy for beautiful and charming people, especially if we can identify with them. We also tend to trust people more if they look similar to us. Even if the suffering is exactly the same for two people, our ability to be empathetic can be biased by a person's appearance. We prefer to help people who are similar to us.

But while empathy may not be perfect, we still need it. Without empathy, we might not help each other at all. The ability to empathize is the foundation of helping, but we need to be aware of the biases that we may bring to our decision making. As we make moral decisions, let's be conscious of what's driving our thinking. Are we being guided by statistics or by anecdotal stories that may be tragic but not representative of the larger reality? We are constantly being influenced through our ability to empathize, whether by advertisements, political campaigns, or Facebook posts. "Let me tell you the story of a little girl who . . ." or "Imagine that you . . ." they say. So, empathy is important to develop, but we need to remember that a story can sometimes blind us to the facts.

We have to be honest. Especially when we know how common fake news and disinformation have become, it's important to cool our jets. Even if some future skill or goal looks invaluable, there are always two sides to every coin. We must be able to see the world through the eyes of others, but we cannot put on rose-colored glasses.

THE BYSTANDER

In the section on "Curiosity and Experimentation," I told the story of the Swedish class where Patrik and I switched names. We had started a downward spiral, and the longer we kept up the charade, the harder it was to alter the situation. Often, we hide behind generalizations, little white lies, and half-truths because it's easier to continue a lie than to stop it.

We live surrounded by so many lies, big and small. If we want to bring real change to the status quo in the future, we will need a capacity for honesty. The world will not change if we go along with the prevailing lies. However, these lies can be hard to detect, because when they're repeated enough, they become normalized, neutral parts of everyday life. This has happened to entire nations historically, but it also happened in that Swedish class. And nothing good ever comes of it.

There were more villains in the story than just Perttu or Patrik. We could never have pulled off that prank if our classmates hadn't gone along with it. It feels like hairsplitting to even try to shift responsibility to anyone else, but silent bystanders are ultimately the ones who allow things to go wrong. And while the actions of teenagers cannot always be generalizable to society at large, this particular analogy does apply to the adult world. Silently standing by and watching injustice is a form of approval when the witnesses could do something about it. They don't understand their own position. They have both the power and the responsibility to be honest with themselves and others. The silence is worse than the scam. Silent onlookers don't want to call attention to injustice, because they fear they will suffer personally as a result.

But if you were caught in a vicious circle like Patrik and me, you would probably want those around you to be honest with you. It might make you angry at first, but ultimately you would thank them. In hard times, we hope to have honest friends around us. Giving honest feedback, comfort, and praise are perhaps the best things we can do with our power of speech.

Challenge yourself to think about what kind of day others are having, and do it without categorizing or labeling. Try, for example, to imagine yourself in someone else's position as you sit on the bus and see so many other different people. This is a first, small step you can take to expand your compassion. The second step is to be honest. Don't be a passive onlooker. When you're having a bad day, you probably hope that someone else will have the ability to be compassionate and honest with you.

FUTURE WORK

- Think about what will best help you be present with other people.

- Be critical of your empathy. Try to be fair!

- Comfort your friend in ways machines can't.

- Be honest about your intentions. Don't play games. Imagine changing places with someone else. How might they feel?

- Be the person others are willing to talk to about sensitive subjects. Always ask this question: "What is it like to be you?"

12

MORAL COURAGE AND ETHICS

Moral courage is a skill that is essential to making the world a better place. It gives us the courage to do what's right.

Our future depends on what kind of moral compass we leave for the next generation. Our entire civilization will be shaped by the ethical thinking of our posterity. Technological development typically involves a range of new ethical problems. Every one of us, whether we work with technology or not, will have to think about our relationship to phones, computers, and other devices. The ever-increasing use of technology has led us to consider the benefits and drawbacks of devices, and most of us don't quite know yet what to think.

We need solid ethics when considering the impacts of technology. From an ethical point of view, it's interesting to consider things such as the impact of social media on privacy, bullying, and news reporting, as well as whether the costs related to addiction and concentration outweigh the benefits of the sharing economy and easy access to information.

Technology can be used in evil, unjust ways. Abuse of new technologies is particularly frightening, because we lack experience with it. Making people see the threats is easy:

artificial intelligence is threatening human jobs, somewhere someone is editing people's genes to make them superhuman, and people who can't keep up with new technologies are being left out of social developments. Of course there's potential dark side to every technology, but as long as ethics guide our actions, we can trust in development being for the common good.

Ethics are timeless, but our problems are new. As a skill for the future, ethical thinking is constantly becoming more important, because we can no longer rely on legislation alone. Laws often lag behind progress, and we can't be sure that the people making the laws will know how to make the right decisions about new technologies because they won't necessarily understand them. These decisions cannot be made in back rooms with a few people discussing what will affect millions.

Technology has made things possible that no one knows how to think about yet. For example, what do you think about gene editing? There isn't a word about it in the UN Declaration on Human Rights, because when that was written in 1948, it wasn't even possible. Now the tools exist, but the ethical standards are still emerging. Article 3 of the declaration enshrines our right to life, liberty, and security of person, and Article 5 prohibits the treatment or punishment of anyone in a cruel, inhuman, or degrading way. Do you think gene editing violates or supports the spirit of the declaration?

Now is the easiest time in history to be a criminal, because new technologies have opened up enormous opportunities to do evil, and the law has not had time to react yet. Bank robberies have evolved into cyberattacks, and now you can do espionage from your couch. Right and wrong don't necessarily go hand in hand with legal and illegal. Situations like this require strong ethical thinking—words—and moral courage—deeds—to stand behind the things that are important to us. We are all responsible for what we accept and what we don't.

WHAT WOULD YOU DO?

A certain police officer had a dog with an incredibly good sense of smell. It was superior to all the other dogs, excelling both at detecting drugs at the airport and finding missing people in the forest. The police decided to clone the dog to save its genes. Now there are two dogs, and they are helping two police officers. Thanks to these dogs, the police can do their work better, and the dogs are saving human lives. What do you think? Did the police act ethically when they cloned this working dog? And could that dog's genes be shared with other cops around the world?

In one small village, on the edge of a secluded lake, there was a lithium mine. It employed virtually all the inhabitants of the village but had recently begun to contaminate the lake, destroying fish and aquatic plants. What should be done? Closing the mine would mean losing jobs and concentrating lithium battery production elsewhere, where the same problems would likely reoccur. Keeping the mine open, on the other hand, would destroy nature and kill the lake. Should we try to preserve nature or jobs? Nature is everyone's responsibility, and the role of one factory is small, but pollution is wrong. Losing a job can be fatal for many families, but we cannot always get back nature once it has been destroyed.

Imagine you're a judge in a courtroom. A sex robot has been raped, and you have to decide whether anything happened that was wrong. The defense attorney says there has been no injustice, because ultimately, it's just a pile of metal that runs on ones and zeros. The prosecutor, on the other hand, argues that the robot has been subjected to acts for which it was not designed and that if such acts and the abuse of robots are allowed, it will become more common and lead to crimes against humans. However, according to the defense lawyer, real people will be spared crimes if the crimes are directed at robots. The prosecutor replies that rape is a reprehensible act in general, and zero tolerance is the only way to eradicate such crimes. As the judge, you listen to the arguments from both sides, after which you must make a judgment. Will you hand down a punishment or not?

The future will bring with it difficult questions. The more aware people are about the ethical challenges associated with technology, the better the world can become. During periods of technological development and norm establishment, the conversations we have can make a huge difference. Even the tiniest corrections to basic issues now will affect the development of future practice, making the situation in ten years very different than it might have been. It's almost like writing a constitution for the ethics of technology.

However, we must also take into consideration that every country may have its own practices. If the Chinese begin modifying the genes of embryos and we don't in Finland, China will gain an advantage, for example, with better learning abilities or stronger resistance to viruses. Even if we think that something is wrong or reprehensible, we still operate in a global world, so will we react to that by allowing genetic editing of humans in Finland as well?

TECHNOLOGY MOVED US FROM THE FRYING PAN INTO THE FIRE

In the nineteenth century, when animal rights activists protested about the living conditions of horses, they never could have imagined that a new technology, the automobile, would improve animal welfare conditions more than all their marches. Thanks to engineers and mechanics, the activists were finally able to breathe a sigh of relief as horse-drawn carriages were exchanged for cars. Technology is often the best way to improve conditions and reduce immediate suffering, even if it may not always seem that way at first.

However, old problems are also replaced by new problems, and often the new problems are worse than the old ones. When cars replaced horses, the horses were freed from their work, but at the same time, cars increased the number and severity of traffic accidents. Globally, more than thirty-five hundred people die in traffic each day, which is an appalling number. Would it have been better to stick to horses? In addition, cars have become a major global polluter, and tackling climate change is a challenge we can't afford to screw up. Would it be smarter to go back to horses? Then the climate activists would be happy, but the animal rights activists would be upset again.

Even when technology makes us a little more ethical, at least ostensibly, it does not completely solve most problems. Debate always remains over whether the old problems were replaced with something better or worse. Hunter-gatherers

did not need to think about ecological concerns or pro-
cessed food, but they did die of starvation and disease. In
the developed world, we have streamlined food production
so we don't die of starvation anymore, but that new efficiency brought with it a novel problem: farm animals, and
the conditions in which they're raised. Activists are needed
to raise awareness so that people can change their behavior
and improve this new animal rights challenge. But the over-
all industry may take an ethical step forward only when we
can make food out of air and create it using bioreactors. It
may be that in the future, biomechanics and chemists will
improve the conditions of livestock and experimental test
animals more than activists ever could. But we have yet to
see what kinds of problems bioreactors bring with them.

Similar developments have taken place with shop-
ping bags. Decades ago, we switched from paper to plastic, because paper bags were believed to destroy forests.
Now plastic bags are destroying the oceans and clogging
our roadsides. Plastic bags have been increasingly replaced
with cloth bags, which are now seen as the best solution.
However, canvas bags require diligent use before enough
benefit accrues to offset the burdens created by their production process. Some people are starting to favor biode-
gradable bags and others are moving back to paper. Activists
do important work, but the situation doesn't always change
for the better, which we often realize only in hindsight.

Remembering the past with nostalgia is easy, but
thankfully the world has been moving forward and we've
made progress on many old ethical problems, for example,
issues related to slavery, human trafficking, and equality.
Now, however, we are facing global threats, and many of

the trends look terrible. Even though modern cars pollute much less than the first automobiles, they still put a greater strain on our atmosphere due to their widespread use. Even though paper or plastic bags were once the best available solution, now too much is too much.

A long life, fulfillment of basic needs, and happiness are now within reach for more people, but at the same time, the size of the population has become a challenge to the carrying capacity of the planet. Or, actually, the lifestyles of rich Westerners, who are depleting the earth's resources, have become a challenge. The richest ten percent produce half of the world's greenhouse gases, but everyone suffers from the results of climate change. We live in a world where we have achieved tremendous advances, but, as if in exchange, we've been given global, existential problems. Would it be better to go back to a hundred years ago, when we didn't need to worry about climate change but many of our basic needs gave us cause for concern?

Let's use this same logic on the future now. What are the significant problems of our time that we're now trying to solve that may cause new, possibly greater challenges in the 2020s and 2030s? For example, artificial intelligence may act like a steroid for problems of inequality in society. A single coder who writes an algorithm that turns out to be racist can cause enormous consequences through millions of devices and apps. We've already seen that biased facial recognition can create systemic discrimination. The problematic piece of code in such situations might have been unintentional, but the repercussions for the people involved can be very concrete, possibly even fatal. When making choices in education, business, or politics, we need to under-

stand the ethical challenges inherent to development and consider the consequences far enough into the future—not just
one school year, one quarter, or one administration at a time.

IT TAKES A VILLAGE TO RAISE A CHILD AND A SOCIETY TO RAISE AN ETHICIST

Ethics are necessary so that productivity and regulations
don't trample common sense. The world needs to be made
better, not just more efficient. Businesses strive to make profits, but when cost-cutting is not optional, ethics are needed
to face difficult choices. So, for example, where do you cut
social services when none of the available options are good?
Because making ethical choices is difficult, we often hide
behind rules and regulations. The resources available often
don't meet the actual demands of the situation, but we still
have to do what we can. The future will require good sense
and responsibility.

It's important that we don't lose sight of our collective
responsibility as a village that raises its children and cares for
its elderly. We cannot allow ourselves to think that we have
no individual responsibility to help others. Even if someone
gets more support from society than you, there's a reason
for that, and it probably has an ethical basis. We need the
ability to take care of each other. Ethics should support your
neighbor, not take things away from them.

We live in a world where polarization occurs on so many
different levels. Economic and technological inequalities
threaten to grow, whether we're talking about individuals,
neighborhoods, cities, or nations. If we turn inward to protect our own well-being, we will tend to regard people in
a weaker position with more indifference. We will ignore

other people's suffering because we'll convince ourselves that we're also the victims of change. In the future, we must be able to make ethically correct choices, because we have a duty to help those in need of assistance.

It's wonderful that in Finland we have been able to give equal opportunities to everyone, regardless of their background. This accomplishment deserves to be praised, but there is a danger in shifting collective responsibility for caring for our neighbors to others—to regulations, laws, and the system. If we don't feel like we're receiving enough support, we blame the system. Maybe the problem isn't just in the system, because in Finland, for example, education and health care equalize the differences between people and place everyone on a nearly level playing field. Perhaps the problem is that we don't all receive strong enough support from our loved ones.

Family, friends, neighbors, and others around us build our foundation. On the other hand, a welfare state is good precisely because when someone is lacking that close-circle support network, the system can support them. But ultimately, we're all responsible for each other. Not the state, the village. Not the system, the society. We must not lose touch with everyday helping, for it's up to all of us to take care of one another.

So how do we know how we're really doing? From the children. The mirror for a society is not its media, but rather those who have been molded in the image of the time. Children's thinking tells us what has been important to our society, i.e., to our village. We teach children to think and we teach them to feel, but are we teaching them how to make the big moral decisions related to humanity and technology? We have a great responsibility to think about the direction in which the value system of the next generation is evolving—to make sure we don't leave behind a morally impoverished society. How we raise the next generation of doctors, scientists, and coders will determine what they make of the future of humanity.

BE THE BUTTERFLY WHOSE FLAPPING WINGS START THE HURRICANE

Change has always started with one person who had the courage to do something morally right even though it was in conflict with the norms of their time. Moral courage has been exemplified by a Black woman who risked punishment by refusing to give up her seat to a white man on a bus in the United States in the 1950s, by a military commander who refused an order to fire his missiles, by a teenage girl who went on strike from school to save the climate, and by a reporter who investigated troll factories and published her findings even though it would make her a target for fake news and other attacks. These people's strong moral compasses guided them to do the right thing, and they will be remembered for it.

In the future, we will need people who have the backbone to do the right thing in difficult situations. People who defend the weak and those who, for whatever reason, are not able to influence their own opportunities. Such actions require increasing courage when our discursive culture tends to be judgmental. However, a strong sense of right and wrong does not preclude contradictions in our thinking. We learned as children that making mistakes is normal and inevitable, but now it feels as if we sometimes forget everything we know about mistakes. People who have made mistakes, especially if the mistake is public, easily become the object of mudslinging, cyberbullying, and psychological abuse even before the facts have been thoroughly checked. We live in a time of double standards, one of which is our attitude toward mistakes. We repeat the mantra that we can learn from our mistakes and yet condemn others for theirs.

One of my friends said he was pretty wild in middle school. Once, when he did something stupid and the teacher demanded an explanation, he decided to play smart aleck. He asked the teacher, "Aren't we supposed to learn from mistakes?" The teacher replied in the affirmative, to which my friend replied that then it was logical to try to make as many mistakes as possible in order to learn as much as possible. The teacher was not amused and once again my friend was sent to sit in the hallway for the rest of the lesson. Well, maybe my friend learned that being impertinent was a new mistake.

The mistakes of public figures are judged with special harshness, and they have no way to take advantage of the situation. Quite the opposite. They have to be perfect in exchange for the attention they receive. They're under such a magnifying glass that we forget they're even people. Defending people who are being bullied is a good example of moral courage, because it requires strong character to stand on the side of the accused under intense pressure.

Correcting injustices begins with the actions of one person, then a second, and finally the support of the majority. Change also happens when people who are not to blame for a problem still take steps to solve it. We need morally courageous people to defend the unwritten rules. Then we can turn them into written rules, i.e., laws that protect us all. Changing the world does not require power, money, or authority, just courage. It's not based on earning awards or advanced degrees. Any of us can start something big and irreversible through acts as small as the fluttering of a butterfly's wings. Bold action creates a domino effect. That is how change has always started.

FUTURE WORK

- Do something that inspires others.

- Delay forming an opinion. Think about the good and bad consequences.

- Set an example to others with your ethical choices.

- Remember that nature does not have a social media profile and cannot update its status itself.

- Dare to act when the situation demands. Encourage others by your own example.

- Keep in mind that individual right choices have always changed the world.

- Do things that your grandparents would be proud of and your grandchildren will be grateful for.

13

AFTER-SCHOOL DETENTION: LOVE

If you want to change the world, you have to know how to love, because only love can make us better people.

"Well, what will they think of next . . . we're supposed to teach love now, are we? You can't teach that! Bah, humbug." For the very reason that the subject arouses such pushback, love should be addressed throughout childhood, adolescence, and adulthood. Even though it's a necessity for our well-being, isn't it strange that it isn't approached systematically at home, at school, or on the job? Something that is so important to us should be cherished. Love helps us through challenges large and small, because it looks to the future. It increases community spirit and care for each other, which we need more of in a globalizing world. And it also encapsulates everything that doesn't otherwise fit into this curriculum, such as peace, forgiveness, and tolerance.

The word *love* is tricky because it is often passed over as a cliché. Everything has already been said about it. But the more important the thing in question, the worse we usually are at talking about it. Love is a sensitive subject, the same way as forgiveness, grace, or holiness. If someone brings it up, we often become confused or shut down. It causes a short circuit because talking about it is so strange. Too squishy, we think. But I think these are commonplace issues that play a significant role in determining our lives, even if we don't know how to talk about them.

We make movies and write novels about love, because what we only understand a little we need to deal with a lot. Love is a topic that can be talked about in the languages of chemistry, society, poetry, biology, music, or religion. Love can also be talked about in terms of forgiveness, grace and holiness, friendship, concern, and caring. All of these things tell us about love in their own way. Romantic love is only one form of it. Love can also be mundane, fading, tenacious, or old, and it can be directed at people, nature, a hobby, or ourselves.

Love is the most important skill of the future, because the only way to make the world better is to learn how to love. You have probably tried to get a friend to change their mind. Did it work by shouting or arguing? And what about showing them studies, quoting experts, or referencing statistics? Maybe someone might change their mind in the face of facts, but facts don't necessarily create a connection between two people. Quite the opposite.

On the other hand, if we can speak with enough honesty that the other person senses the love behind our words, they listen. We only start reevaluating our actions once we realize that the other person is speaking from their heart. Love is the only way to get another person to change their ways. Conflict can be overcome only through love. I believe that this applies equally to global negotiations, conflicts, and crisis aid. If we could learn to love better, there would be less sorrow in the world. If we want to change the world, first we must learn how to love.

WHAT IS LOVE?

I think friendship today is pretty much the same thing it was a hundred years ago. It's about caring, common interests, and loyalty. Not much significant has changed about sibling relationships, either, because bickering, caring, and shared experiences continue to characterize that dynamic. But romantic love and couples' relationships have experienced a significant upheaval if we compare the current situation to a century ago. This includes: how we find partners; who qualifies as a partner in the first place; what expectations we have for relationships; what marriage means; at what age people start families; and what protocols, formalities, and gender roles there are. Between 2005 and 2012, more than one-third of couples who married in the United States originally met online or through a dating app. What was once completely unheard of is now common.

The expression of romantic love is in transition. In Finland, the divorce rate grew dramatically at the end of the 1980s, after which it has remained steady—yet we divorce more than average compared to other countries. We invest more in love in the form of apps, experiences, and purchases than ever before, but we marry less. Something has happened, but what and why?

Romantic love has caught a virus, and we're starting to develop a cough. Perhaps the biggest influence on our conception of love is the media. We cannot deny the impact of television shows, celebrity couple interviews, and romantic comedies on us, at least subconsciously. Advertising and branding have also gotten in on the act, since love sells well. Advertising slogans and images try to access that uncertain part of us that wishes it could buy love. Love has acquired all the hallmarks of a commodity, as if it were a product. We have embraced the idea that love should always feel new, fascinating, and exciting, like a great sale or opening a new package. If we could be content with the mundane and functional, we might not always be looking for something new and shiny.

Investing in long-term love requires turning something very ordinary into something special. We are now freer to choose comfort and emotion, but perhaps that's why we're so lost. Now comfort and emotion are also guiding us to places they didn't before. We have internalized what has been advertised to us: romantic love looks and feels a certain way. Before it was a service, but now it is a product. Service involves collaboration, purpose, and helping, while products involve novelty, status, and ownership. We want something uncomplicated, easy, and well reviewed.

We often say to people who are looking for a partner that there are plenty of fish in the sea. Perhaps the transformation of love is like climate change, which is increasing the temperature of the sea. Now fish have to survive in an altered environment, which doesn't suit them as well as it used to. Likewise, we must adapt to the era of modern romantic love.

However, it's also good to remember that although there were fewer divorces before, that doesn't necessarily mean people were happy. There's plenty of evidence of marital discord in correspondence from 1950s Finland, where elderly farm housewives and city ladies mourned their lost lives and the terrible husbands that they had no way of divorcing at the time. There are always two sides to every coin, and when we're making generalizations about love, we have to remember that every story is different.

LOVE IN HOLLYWOOD

It was a Friday night, and I was lying in bed, tired from another week. Suddenly a call interrupted my smartphone scrolling, and I was surprised to see the name of an old friend. I'd last seen them on my previous trip to Los Angeles, about a year earlier. My friend said hi and asked in a strange voice how I was doing. When I asked how they were doing in return, they burst into tears and began a confused account of how terrible things were for them. They had noticed from social media that I was in town and asked if I could come visit. Even though it was a long way from Marina del Rey to Hollywood, I headed out.

The crying was about romantic troubles. We talked through things, and as evening turned to night, it seemed like everything was handled—my friend seemed like themself again. Even so, I stayed the night because I wanted to be sure that everything would still be fine in the morning. And besides, the trip back to my apartment would have taken more than an hour.

During the night I woke up to strange sounds. My friend was alternately laughing and crying, so I got off the couch and went to see what was up. I found them with a knife in their hand. It was like I was in a Hollywood thriller in real life. I approached carefully and took away the knife. Then I set it on top of a high cupboard they couldn't reach. My friend was not the person I knew. They listened to me, but it felt like I was just as powerless as they were. I remember comforting them as well as I could, but I don't remember a word of what I said.

The noise woke the other residents of the house, so I also had other people to back me up. We called the police, because we didn't know what else we could do. My friend had to go vomit, and it turned out they had taken an overdose of some medication. Everything was very confusing. The police came, and even though my friend resisted at first, they seemed to feel relieved after getting in the police car. The police took my friend to the hospital, and I went back to sleep, praying that they would pull through everything. The next day, my friend was released from the hospital, and we arranged to meet at the beach. We sat on the sand and listened to the pounding of the waves. It seemed like something had just been removed from them, and they were themself again. They looked out at the horizon, and we were both silent.

There are certain things you never forget. These include situations when we don't know what to do. We're taught to cope with everyday challenges and tasks, but do we know how to speak to others in times of need?

My friend's story gave me the following lesson: if you love someone, it's better to show them than just to tell them. But if you don't love someone anymore, it's best to say it than to show it. Love makes us do wonderful things, but it also makes us do terrible things. I believe that similar situations could be prevented if we addressed love and related themes more together. Everyone involved would be grateful for that.

CAN LOVE BE TAUGHT?

Broken hearts and romantic complications are part of life. Who among us has never hurt someone else or been hurt at some point in our lives? Even though broken hearts are common and affect everyone's ability to function, we often keep them to ourselves. Why don't we approach love systematically and logically in the place where we learn all the other basics of life? Love should be dealt with from the perspectives of history, the media, and entertainment, as well as society.

Before, each individual knew the members of their community. If something happened in a village or a tribe, everyone knew it. Arguments were just as audible through thin walls or huts as the silence or reconciliation afterward. Now you can have friends tell you they're getting divorced without ever having had the slightest clue that anything was wrong. Love has become a private thing that happens behind closed doors. And often, rather than divorcing because we're unhappy, it's because we think that we could be happier.

The polished lives of social media make us think that there's always something better out there to find. When there are enough options, nothing is satisfying anymore. The issue isn't about us being sad. The issue is about us being sold a lie about something better. In a village community, this phenomenon could never develop, and in the future, we will need to remind ourselves of that. What we imagine about other couples that we see online and in the media is only what we imagine. We can't know the reality.

We need to react to this changing environment. If we don't teach commitment, selflessness, compassion, and consideration for others to children, we can't expect that kind of behavior from adults. The golden rule can also be applied to education and work. Do unto children in school as you would have them do unto you in the workplace. Unfortunately, many of the most significant things in life have been left to us to learn alone. The school of hard knocks is expected to teach us everything that real school doesn't, but this does not need to be the case.

Love is a skill just like any other, because it can be learned and improved. Love encompasses many other things, which is why it can feel like a difficult subject. But at its core, it is about selflessness. This is the essence of humanity. In a world that emphasizes individualism, placing others ahead of ourselves will be an invaluable skill in the future. Every situation, moment, and encounter can teach us something about love if we are sensitized to see love as a skill. The future will need people who actively pay attention to love. However, if love is not seen as a skill, we will not learn from our mistakes.

The very first lessons in love we get at home, but schools could build on that. For example, if they taught love in after-school detention, we might see the number of detentions decrease. We might also see detention become popular. Family and friends are also important to the development of this skill. In all teaching and learning situations, we must touch the heart before we can touch the head. There is a wise saying that is attributed to Aristotle, although it can't be factually traced back to his works. "Educating the mind without educating the heart is no education at all." Love can be taught. It must be taught.

WHAT DID HE BUILD?

Once I heard a story that claimed that in Finnish we used to use the word *rakettaa* instead of the modern *rakentaa* to mean "to build." When a young couple was married, it was customary to receive a dowry, in which the bride's family gave a gift to the groom's family—sort of like a wedding gift for the family. In a country like Finland, it was often simplest to transport the gift to the groom's family by water. Because the gifts were often large, they would have to knock together a new boat to move it. Sometimes two boats, in fact, which were connected by a piece of wood. This piece of wood had no name, but because it was something they had to build, *rakettaa* back then, a new noun was created to describe it: *rakkaus*.

As this word became a part of the general language, it also began to take on new meanings. Since two lovers were being joined together when a *rakkaus* was built, the word gradually began to shift from the piece of wood to the feeling between the people. So originally our word for love meant a piece of wood that was built to connect two boats together. It was like a bond that was supposed to keep the two people together on their journey toward new horizons. Who knows if this story is actually true, but the idea is at least inspiring.

Love is needed to maintain important human relationships, like that piece of wood connecting two boats. The future will bring waves and currents. The ongoing upheavals in everything from education to transportation and from health care to nutrition will affect the lives of each and every person. Inequality will inevitably arise, as it already has. This is when we will most need love, that joining piece of wood, to keep different people united with each other. Tolerance and acceptance will be central to those boats not diverging in the waves. We must not shut anyone out if we hope to hold on to our communities. This can put us all on the same side, even if we do have differences between us.

Perhaps in the future we will need to do work like the carpenters who built those pieces of wood to join those boats. But our work will be taking others into consideration, nurturing community, and building peace. Love cannot be outsourced to a system, a machine, or technology. It will be left up to us. Many of the skills suggested in this book culminate in love: self-knowledge, compassion, patience, honesty, persistence, and communication.

As I observed in the introduction, work has moved from our muscles to our heads, and from our heads to our hearts. Once machines have replaced muscle power and computers have replaced brainpower, the education of the heart will become paramount. We have come full circle and found again that we cannot fight the efficiency of machines. The breakneck pace of technological development has brought us back to the basics. Machines cannot love. It is impossible to automate a person who does things for love. Compassion is the ultimate coding challenge. Anyone who can love will be an incomparable robot in the future. And perhaps that is as it should be.

CONCLUSION:
WHEN NOTHING IS
CERTAIN, EVERYTHING
IS POSSIBLE

believe that by developing the skills of the future outlined in this book, we will succeed in the coming decades. However, there's one thing that I think is especially essential to success. As discussed in earlier chapters, we need collaboration between people of different ages in order to find our way. What storytelling, creativity, entrepreneurship, or love are for young people and old people might not match up. We need intergenerational dialogue.

As innovation accelerates, it will take only a few years for the surroundings two people grew up in to look nothing alike. This can create situations in which people of different ages operate using differing words, terms, concepts, and ideas. Once when I was visiting a friend of mine, the family's nine-year-old daughter reported with her eyes all aglow that she wanted a factory for her desk for her birthday. We were all a little confused until someone realized that she was probably talking about a 3-D printer. It makes toys like a factory and can fit on a desk. But even though we'd found the right term, the grandmother still didn't understand what kind of gadget we were talking about. She didn't quite know how to respond to the girl's enthusiasm.

We can't afford to fail to understand the world in which children and young people are growing up. The future needs dialogue and mentoring between people of different ages. The older generation has experience—which younger people literally cannot yet have. However, young people have many insights, because they've grown up with the internet and are native to this new millennium. Both have something special to offer. Older people know what has remained the same despite previous revolutions and will probably continue to, but the young know what needs to change. We need to learn how to build on the things that are permanent and take into account the things that are evolving.

We know that change will happen more quickly in the future than in the past. Only a couple of generations ago, it was still typical for parents and their children to have quite similar lives. If you are a parent now, the life of your children will not be at all the same as your life. You will have to be careful with advice based on your own experiences. It wouldn't make sense to give instructions that worked in the past but will not in the future. It wouldn't make sense to pass on habits of thought that are stuck in the ideals of the past. That's the opposite of teaching and raising a child.

As a result of this, many of our everyday assumptions will need to be redefined. What was expected of a civilized person thirty years ago is different from today's expectations. A business executive or a neighbor with a popular YouTube channel can now have more influence than political leaders. Money has changed form, ownership has experienced a revolution, and privacy meant a different thing in the 1970s than it does now. Times have changed.

The internet, the computer, and the smartphone have made my years growing up very different from my parents'. However, it's thrilling to think that we will experience many more revolutions of the same magnitude in the coming decades. Maybe five. Maybe ten. They may have to do with artificial intelligence, synthetic biology, 3-D printing, virtual reality, robotics, quantum computing, blockchain technology, or something we don't know anything about yet.

The life of each generation is unique, and neither past nor future generations can fully comprehend this alone. We must take time to reflect on big questions with people of all ages. My grandparents were in their twenties in the 1950s, and my nephew will be twenty in the 2040s. When I see them playing together and contemplate their life paths, it feels like I'm in a time machine.

Think of the world where your parents, your grandparents, your great-grandparents, and their parents were born. Developments over a hundred years are very concrete. Previous generations have left behind something better than what they received. Through their work, they provided the next generation with a better starting point. What kind of legacy will we leave behind? Many teens and young adults believe that the next generation will only be left with huge problems to solve, and because of this many of them are thinking twice about having children. How did we fail to continue developing and only create global challenges to heap on the rising generation? We're good at measuring activity, but inactivity is difficult to evaluate. What is the price of what we are leaving undone?

If we listen to young people's hopes, dreams, and concerns, they won't find the future so distressing. It's also good to remember that worldwide, one of every two people is under the age of thirty, and every fourth person is under fourteen. This is the age group that will soon be overrepresented in the workforce. Out in the world, it will be their needs that will guide the development of industries in ten to twenty years. Because the age distribution is reversed in some developed countries, like where I live in Finland, there is a danger that we won't listen enough to the young.

The year 1995 is just as far from 2020 as is 2045. Many people currently in management positions will retire over the next ten years. If we don't involve the coming generation in decision making, we will be making decisions in a bubble that is not representative of the future. We should give the people who will create the future a chance. Let us remember the words of the late Kofi Annan: "You are never too young to lead. And we are never too old to learn."

We need to pay attention to how we talk about the future and what kind of picture we give of it to young people. For example, we often describe the future as uncertain, but I want to challenge us all to think about what that actually means. When we say uncertainty, "un-certainty," we are trying to explain something through its opposite. Would you understand what milk is if I said it was nonjuice? Imagine if I meant to say I was walking. Would I tell you that I was unflying, nonrunning, or antiswimming? You wouldn't have a clue what I was talking about even though I'd just given you a list of descriptions. We can't talk about the future by saying it's uncertain, that it's hard to describe, and that it's approaching at an accelerating pace. We need to try to understand better the phenomena behind these words.

Predicting the future is by definition an impossible task, but when we add to the equation the difficulty of describing what we do know, it becomes even more challenging. That is why it's critically important for every parent, teacher, and journalist to think about what kind of vision we're reinforcing about the future. We need to talk about skills and employment, but it's misleading to say that machines are replacing people and that all the jobs will disappear. *Replacing* and *disappearing* are very absolute, negative-sounding words. It's all just change. New circumstances. A new normal that we'll need to get used to. Every generation has left behind a different world, and our job is to continue that.

Ultimately, talking about the future requires imagination. It can make us hopeful for a better tomorrow or cynical in times of great upheaval. There is climate anxiety, the global refugee crisis, and the threat of mass unemployment. The future of Europe hangs in the balance, the middle class is rising in Asia and Africa, and the power dynamics between the United States, China, and Russia are in flux. The greater the change we are living through, the more we fear the unknown. We need restraint, but we can't underestimate the threats we face. We have to be precise with our facts so that trivialities don't steal our attention and eat us alive. My skydiving experience taught me that anything—a thought, a comment, or a situation—can get stuck in the back of our minds and haunt us, affecting everything we do.

It would be good to keep in mind that technology is a huge help, but it doesn't make problems go away. As suffering, deprivation, and evil are reduced in the world, that doesn't necessarily mean that we become any happier. Instead, we just get upset about smaller and smaller things. Our attention just shifts to different problems. Therefore, it's important that we talk about the future prudently and build faith in our own abilities. If someone asks you what you think about the future, I have an answer for you. Say, "I can't wait!"

Many people fear the change in the world, because the media and fictional dystopias have programmed them with a negative idea of the future. Unfortunately, we project our fears forward, including into our children. We are a curious and playful species that invents tools and builds technology that belongs to everyone. But spreading nightmare visions of the future can turn us against each other. Social media provides unfortunate events with an unprecedented audience, allowing isolated incidents to fill us with concern. These stories make us reserved, defensive, and easily provoked. But what we feel does not always reflect reality.

What do we do to prevent a frightening future from paralyzing us? The best way to keep fears at bay is to live in the here and now, actively interacting with others. A person who is present in the moment doesn't try to escape into daydreams and is rarely afraid, because they don't let their imagination play tricks on them. The future is not going to wash over us in an uncontrollable wave. The future is exactly what we do today for tomorrow. It will not be frightening if we build it together.

In the chapter on "Technology and the Future," I talked about the ways that technology helps people do things when our own abilities come up short. Machines do many tasks better than we do, but they don't make us better people. Machines don't teach us right and wrong. The more we let machines think for us, the less we will think about our own good. Technology makes us powerful, but it doesn't change who we are or tell us what we should do. Technological innovation is accelerating, but human growth is not. That is a very steady process. People are easier to make powerful than kind. Someone can become a celebrity quickly, but becoming attentive takes much more time. It is possible that technology will turn us into something we don't like.

We're living at an inflection point. We can build fantastic solutions using technology. We can revolutionize education, health care, eating, living, and traveling. We can explore the entire universe around us, from the smallest cells to the largest galaxies. But if years from now we find that we haven't done all that for the sake of humanity, it won't matter. We will have done it all for nothing. Technology can be used for good only if we ourselves are good. I want to believe that the future will do us a favor. That we will be able to become better.

The skills discussed in this book are goals that will make the future more humane. They will help us to have the courage to step into the unknown, even if we're afraid. The future is always a risk, but risk is essential for development. We don't conquer fear with wit or intelligence, we overcome it by educating our hearts. So, take the risk and open yourself to the future. Jump into the unknown.

SOURCES

BBC News, "Myanmar profile – Timeline," BBC, September 3, 2018, https://www.bbc.com/news/world-asia-pacific-12992883.

The Berkeley Innovation Index. https://berkeleyinnovationindex .org.

Bloom, Paul, *Against Empathy: The Case for Rational Compassion*. London: The Bodley Head, 2016.

Cacioppo, John T., Stephanie Cacioppo, Gian C. Gonzaga, Elizabeth L. Ogburn & Tyler J. VanderWeele, "Marital Satisfaction and Breakups Differ Across Online and Offline Meeting Venues," *Proceedings of the National Academy of Sciences* 110 (25), 10135–10140, June 3, 2013, https://doi.org/10.1073/pnas.1222447110.

Carton, Andrew M, 2018, "'I'm Not Mopping the Floors, I'm Putting a Man on the Moon': How NASA Leaders Enhanced the Meaningfulness of Work by Changing the Meaning of Work," *Administrative Science Quarterly* 63 (2), 323–369, https://doi .org/10.1177/0001839217713748.

Cartwright, Mark, "Athenian Democracy," *Ancient History Encyclopedia*, April 3, 2018, https://www.ancient.eu/Athenian_Democ racy/.

Castrén, Paavo, *Antiikin myytit* ("Myths of Antiquity"), Helsinki: Otava, 2017.

Central Intelligence Agency, "Burma," The World Factbook, 2019, https://www.cia.gov/the-world-factbook/countries/burma/.

Crouch, Tom D, "Wright brothers," *Encyclopædia Britannica*, 2018, https://www.britannica.com/biography/Wright-brothers.

Cyranoski, David & Heidi Ledford, "Genome-edited baby claim

provokes international outcry," *Nature* 563 (7733), 607–608, 2018, https://doi.org/10.1038/d41586-018-07545-0.

Dauch, Carly, Michelle Imwalle, Brooke Ocasio & Alexia E. Metz, "The influence of the number of toys in the environment on toddlers' play," *Infant Behavior and Development* 50, 78–87, 2018, https://doi.org/10.1016/j.infbeh.2017.11.005.

Einstein, Albert. Letter to Carl Seelig March 11, 1952, Einstein Archives 39-013, The Hebrew University of Jerusalem, http://www.albert-einstein.org. Letter also available at https://library.ethz.ch/en/locations-and-media/platforms/einstein-online/princeton-1933-1955.html.

Ei Shwe Phyu, "Myanmar's basic education curriculum gets a make-over," *Myanmar Times*, March 9, 2017, https://www.mmtimes.com/special-features/231-educentre/25297-myanmar-s-basic-education-curriculum-gets-a-makeover.html.

The Elders, "Kofi Annan," 2018, https://theelders.org/profile/kofi-annan.

FAO, IFAD, UNICEF, WFP & WHO. "The State of Food Security and Nutrition in the World 2019. Safeguarding against economic slowdowns and downturns." Rome: FAO, http://www.fao.org/3/ca5162en/ca5162en.pdf.

Festinger, Leon, "A Theory of Social Comparison Processes," In *Social Comparison Theories. Key Readings in Social Psychology*, eds. Diedrik A. Stapel & Hart Blanton, New York: Psychology Press, 2007, 29–44. (Original article published 1954.)

Gore, Timothy, "Extreme Carbon Inequality," Oxfam International, 2015, https://oxf.am/2FMYtY2.

Gottfried, Jeffrey & Elizabeth Grieco, "Younger Americans are better than older Americans at telling factual news statements from opinions," Pew Research Center, October 23, 2018, https://pewrsr.ch/2NXnRgI.

Guess, Andrew, Jonathan Nagler & Joshua Tucker, "Less than you think: Prevalence and predictors of fake news dissemination on Facebook," *Science Advances* 5 (1), 2019, https://doi.org/10.1126/sciadv.aau4586.

Haas, Benjamin, "Chinese man 'marries' robot he built himself," *The Guardian*, April 4, 2017, https://www.theguardian.com/world/2017/apr/04/chinese-man-marries-robot-built-himself.

Hall, Mark, "Facebook," *Encyclopædia Britannica*, 2019, https://www.britannica.com/topic/Facebook.

Healey, Aleeya, Alan Mendelsohn & Council on Early Childhood, "Selecting Appropriate Toys for Young Children in the Digital Era," *Pediatrics* 143 (1), 2018, https://doi.org/10.1542/peds.2018-3348.

Hedberg, Mimosa, "Suomi oli 100 vuotta sitten kehitysmaa—näin se vertautuu nykymaailmaan." ("One hundred years ago Finland was a developing country—see how it compares to the modern world.") *Fingo ry*, May 12, 2017, https://www.fingo.fi/ajankohtaista/uutiset/suomi-oli-100-vuotta-sitten-kehitysmaa-nain-severtautuu-nykymaailmaan.

Hukkinen, Juhana, "Miksi maailmankaupan kasvu on hidastunut?" ("Why has world trade growth slowed?") *Talous ja Yhteiskunta*, April 2016, http://www.labour.fi/ty/tylehti/ty/ty42016/ty42016pdf/ty42016Hukkinen.pdf.

International Labour Organization, "World Employment and Social Outlook," 2019, https://www.ilo.org/wesodata.

International Telecommunication Union, "Global ICT developments 2001–2018," 2019, https://www.itu.int/en/ITU-D/Statistics/Pages/stat/default.aspx.

Iyengar, Sheena, "How to make choosing easier," TED talk, 2011, https://www.ted.com/talks/sheena_iyengar_choosing_what_to_choose/transcript?language=en.

Johnson, Steve, "Global unemployment hits lowest point for 4 decades." *Financial Times*, June 12, 2018, https://www.ft.com/content/1e8f4cf4-f257-11e8-ae55-df4bf40f9d0d.

Kaku, Michio, "Albert Einstein," *Encyclopædia Britannica*, 2019, https://www.britannica.com/biography/Albert-Einstein.

Lucas, Gale M., Jonathan Gratch, Aisha King & Louis-Philippe Morency, "It's only a computer: Virtual humans increase willingness to disclose," *Computers in Human Behavior* 37, 94–100, 2014, https://doi.org/10.1016/j.chb.2014.04.043.

Mathers, Colin D. & Dejan Loncar, "Projections of global mortality and burden of disease from 2002 to 2030," *PLoS Medicine* 3 (11), 2006, https://doi.org/10.1371/journal.pmed.0030442.

McCabe, Eamonn, "Photojournalist Kevin Carter dies," *The Guardian*, July 30, 2014, https://www.theguardian.com/media/2014/jul/30/kevin-carter-photojournalist-obituary-archive-1994.

Murphy, Julia & Max Roser, "Internet," Our World in Data, 2019, https://ourworldindata.org/internet.

Myanmar Ministry of Labour, Immigration and Population, "2014

Myanmar Population and Housing Census," Policy Brief on Education, 2014, https://myanmar.unfpa.org/sites/default/files/pub-pdf/policy%20brief%20and%20infographics_Education.pdf.

Müller, Barbara C. N., Matthijs L. Van Leeuwen, Rick B. Van Baaren, Harold Bekkering & A. P. Dijksterhuis, "Empathy is a beautiful thing: Empathy predicts imitation only for attractive others," *Scandinavian Journal of Psychology* 54 (5), 2013, 401–406, https://doi.org/10.1111/sjop.12060.

National Association for the Education of Young Children, n.d., "What the Research Says: Impact of Specific Toys on Play," https://www.naeyc.org/resources/topics/play/specific-toys-play.

Oleson, T. J., "Bjarni Herjólfsson," *Dictionary of Canadian Biography*, vol. 1. University of Toronto/Université Laval, 2003–2019, 1979, http://www.biographi.ca/en/bio/bjarni_herjolfsson_1E.html.

———. "Leifr Eiriksson," *Dictionary of Canadian Biography*, vol. 1. University of Toronto/Université Laval, 2003–2019, 1979, http://www.biographi.ca/en/bio/leifr_eiriksson_1E.html.

Organisation for Economic Co-operation and Development, "Marriage and divorce rates," 2019, https://www.oecd.org/social/family/SF_3_1_Marriage_and_divorce_rates.pdf.

Ortiz-Ospina, Esteban & Max Roser, "Happiness and Life Satisfaction," *Our World in Data*, 2017, https://ourworldindata.org/happiness-and-life-satisfaction.

Pajarinen, Mika & Petri Rouvinen, "Computerization Threatens One Third of Finnish Employment," *ETLA Muistio* 22, January 31, 2014, http://pub.etla.fi/ETLA-Muistio-Brief-22.pdf.

Penrose, Roland, *Picasso: His Life and Work*, third ed., London: Granada, 1981.

Rice-Oxley, Mark, "Mental illness: is there really a global epidemic?" *The Guardian*, June 3, 2019, https://www.theguardian.com/society/2019/jun/03/mental-illness-is-there-really-a-global-epidemic.

Rizzo, Albert "Skip" and Russell Shilling, "Clinical Virtual Reality tools to advance the prevention, assessment, and treatment of PTSD," *European Journal of Psychotraumatology* 8, sup. 5, 2017, https://doi.org/10.1080/20008198.2017.1414560.

Robinson, Gwen, "Myanmar: Opening up," *Financial Times*, April 18, 2012, https://www.ft.com/content/28f72a96-7e40-11e1-b20a-00144feab49a.

————. "Myanmar opens telecoms to foreign groups," *Financial Times*, January 15, 2013, https://www.ft.com/content/3ade6302-5ef8 -11e2-9f18-00144feab49a.

Ronson, Jon, "How One Stupid Tweet Blew Up Justine Sacco's Life," *The New York Times Magazine*, February 12, 2015, https:// www.nytimes.com/2015/02/15/magazine/how-one-stupid -tweet-ruined-justine-saccos-life.html.

Roser, Max, "Twice as long—life expectancy around the world" *Our World in Data*, 2019, https://ourworldindata.org/life-expec- tancy-globally.

————. "War and Peace," *Our World in Data*, 2019, https://ourworld indata.org/war-and-peace.

Roser, Max & Esteban Ortiz-Ospina, "Global Extreme Poverty," *Our World in Data*, 2017, https://ourworldindata.org/extreme -poverty.

Sadie, Stanley, "Wolfgang Amadeus Mozart," *Encyclopædia Britan- nica*, 2019, https://www.britannica.com/biography/Wolfgang -Amadeus-Mozart.

Seneca, Lucius Annaeus, *Letters from a Stoic*, translated by Robin Campbell, London: Penguin Books, 1969.

Subedar, Anisa, "The country where Facebook posts whipped up hate," BBC, September 12, 2018, https://www.bbc.com/news /blogs-trending-45449938.

Svenska Yle, "Nytt världsrekord i Finland," *Yleisradio Oy*, July 3, 2004, https://svenska.yle.fi/artikel/2004/07/03/nytt-varld srekord-i-finland.

Tanskanen, Jari, "Suomessa onnistuttiin valmistamaan proteiinia ilmasta—mullistava keksintö voi olla yksi ratkaisu maailman ruokapulaan" ("Finland succeeded in making protein from the air—a revolutionary invention may be one solution to the world's food shortages."), *Yleisradio Oy*, June 17, 2019, https://yle.fi/uuti set/3-10833123.

Tapscott, Don, *Grown Up Digital: How the Net Generation is Changing Your World*, New York: McGraw Hill Education, 2008.

Tikkanen, Amy, "William Lee," *Encyclopædia Britannica*, 2019, https://www.britannica.com/biography/William-Lee.

Traïni, Christophe, *The Animal Rights Struggle. An Essay in Historical Sociology*, translated by Richard Jemmett, Amsterdam: Amster- dam University Press, 2016, https://doi.org/10.5117/978908 9648495.

Trautwein, Catherine, "Myanmar third for mobile growth," *Myanmar Times*, July 15, 2015, https://www.mmtimes.com/business/technology/15514-myanmar-third-for-mobile-growth.html.

UN News, "'Global clarion call' for youth to shape efforts to forge peace in the most dangerous combat zones," United Nations, March 6, 2019, https://news.un.org/en/story/2019/03/1034211.

United Nations Department of Economic and Social Affairs, Population Division, "Profiles of Ageing 2019," 2019, https://population.un.org/ProfilesOfAgeing2019/index.html.

United Nations Development Programme, "Human Development Data (1990–2017). Education Index," 2018, http://hdr.undp.org/en/data#.

Vettenranta, Jouni, Jouni Välijärvi, Arto Ahonen, Jarkko Hautamäki, Jenna Hiltunen, Kaisa Leino, Suvi Lähteinen, Kari Nissinen, Virva Nissinen, Eija Puhakka, Juhani Rautopuro, and Mari-Pauliina Vainikainen, *Pisa 15 ensituloksia. Huipulla pudotuksesta huolimatta.* ("PISA 25 Preliminary Results: Still at the Top Despite a Drop"), Finnish Ministry of Education and Culture Publications 2016: 41, 2016, http://julkaisut.valtioneuvosto.fi/bitstream/handle/10024/79052/okm41.pdf?sequence=1&isAllowed=y.

Voorhies, James, "Pablo Picasso (1881–1973)," *Heilbrunn Timeline of Art History*, New York: The Metropolitan Museum of Art, 2004, http://www.metmuseum.org/toah/hd/pica/hd_pica.htm.

Väestöliitto, "Avioerot" ("Divorces"), *Statistics from 1970–2014*, https://www.vaestoliitto.fi/tieto_ja_tutkimus/vaestontutkimuslaitos/tilastoja/parisuhteet_ja_seksuaalisuus/avioerot/.

Välijärvi, Jouni, Pekka Kupari, Arto K. Ahonen, Inga Arffman, Heidi Harju Luukkainen, Kaisa Leino, Markku Niemivirta, Kari Nissinen, Katariina Salmela-Aro, Mirja Tarnanen, Heta Tuominen-Soini, Jouni Vettenranta, and Raimo Vuorinen, *Millä eväillä osaaminen uuteen nousuun? PISA 2012 -tutkimustuloksia* ("How to Rise Again? PISA 2012 Research Results"), Finnish Ministry of Education and Culture Publications 2015: 6, http://urn.fi/URN:ISBN:978-952-263-334-7.

Wittgenstein, Ludwig, *Culture and Value*, eds. G. H. von Wright & Heikki Nyman, translated by Peter Winch, Oxford: Blackwell, 1980.

The World Bank, "The World Bank in China," 2019, https://www.worldbank.org/en/country/china/overview.